MALCOLM X

Another Side of the Movement

The History of the
Civil Rights Movement

MALCOLM X

Another Side of the Movement

by Mark Davies

With an Introduction by
ANDREW YOUNG

Silver Burdett Press

These words are dedicated to the memory of Steven Biko

The author is indebted to Alex Haley and his book *The Autobiography of Malcolm X* for information regarding Malcolm X's early years. He would also like to express his gratitude to Dr. Betty Shabazz, Sule Greg Wilson, Professor Aldon Morris, and Della Rowland, all of whose contributions and inspiration helped shape the book and enlighten the author.

Series Consultant: Aldon Morris

Cover and Text Design: Design Five, New York
Maps: General Cartography, Inc.
Series Editorial Supervisor: Richard G. Gallin
Series Supervision of Art and Design: Leslie Bauman
Series Editing: Agincourt Press
Developmental Editor: Della Rowland

Consultants: James Marion Gray, Ph.D., Teacher, Lincoln Park High School, Lincoln Park, Michigan; Catherine J. Lenix–Hooker, Deputy Chief, Schomburg Center for Research in Black Culture, New York Public Library.

Permissions and photo credits appear on page 130.

Library of Congress Cataloging-in-Publication Data

Davies, Mark.
    Malcolm X: another side of the movement / by Mark Davies; with an introduction by Andrew Young.
        p.   cm. —(The History of the civil rights movement)
    Includes bibliographical references and index.
    Summary: A biography of the African American who led a movement to unite black people throughout the world.
    1. X, Malcolm, 1925-1965—Juvenile literature.   2. Black Muslims—Biography—Juvenile literature.   3. Afro-Americans—Biography—Juvenile literature.
[1. X, Malcolm, 1925-1965.   2. Afro-Americans—Biography.]   I. Title. II. Series.
BP223.Z8L5733   1990
297'.87'092—dc20
[B]
[92]
ISBN 0-382-09925-7 (lib. bdg.)   90-32003
ISBN 0-382-24063-4 (pbk.)   CIP
                                                   AC

CONTENTS

INTRODUCTION

By Andrew Young

Some thirty years ago, a peaceful revolution took place in the United States, as African Americans sought equal rights. That revolution, which occurred between 1954 and 1968, is called the civil rights movement. Actually, African Americans have been struggling for their civil rights for as long as they have been in this country. Before the Civil War, brave abolitionists were calling out for an end to the injustice and cruelty of slavery. Even after the Civil War freed slaves, African Americans were still forced to fight other forms of racism and discrimination—segregation and prejudice. This movement still continues today as people of color battle racial hatred and economic exploitation all over the world.

The books in this series tell the stories of the lives of Ella Baker, Stokely Carmichael, Fannie Lou Hamer, Jesse Jackson, Malcolm X, Thurgood Marshall, Rosa Parks, A. Philip Randolph, and Martin Luther King, Jr.—just a few of the thousands of brave people who worked in the civil rights movement. Learning about these heroes is an important lesson in American history. They risked their homes and their jobs—and some gave their lives—to secure rights and freedoms that we now enjoy and often take for granted.

Most of us know the name of Dr. Martin Luther King, Jr., the nonviolent leader of the movement. But others who were just as important may not be as familiar. Rosa Parks insisted on her right to a seat on a public bus. Her action started a bus boycott that changed a segregation law and sparked a movement.

Ella Baker was instrumental in founding two major civil rights organizations, the Southern Christian Leadership Conference (SCLC) and the Student Nonviolent Coordinating Committee (SNCC). One of the chairpersons of SNCC, Stokely Carmichael, is perhaps best known for making the slogan "Black Power" famous. Malcolm X, the strong voice from the urban north, rose from a prison inmate to a powerful black Muslim leader.

Not many people know that the main organizer of the 1963 March on Washington was A. Philip Randolph. Younger leaders called Randolph the "father of the movement." Fannie Lou Hamer, a poor sharecropper from Mississippi, was such a powerful speaker for voters rights that President Lyndon Johnson blocked out television coverage of the 1964 Democratic National Convention to keep her off the air. Thurgood Marshall was the first African American to be made a Supreme Court justice.

Many who demanded equality paid for their actions. They were fired from their jobs, thrown out of their homes, beaten, and even killed. But they marched, went to jail, and put their lives on the line over and over again for the right to equal justice. These rights include something as simple as being able to sit and eat at a lunch counter. They include political rights such as the right to vote. They also include the equal rights to education and job opportunities that lead to economic betterment.

We are now approaching a level of democracy that allows all citizens of the United States to participate in the American dream. Jesse Jackson, for example, has pursued the dream of the highest office in this land, the president of the United States. Jackson's running for president was made possible by those who went before him. They are the people whose stories are included in this biography and history series, as well as thousands of others who remain nameless. They are people who depend upon you to carry on the dream of liberty and justice for all people of the world.

Civil Rights Movement Time Line

—1954— —1955— —1956— —1957—

May 17—
Brown v. *Board of Education of Topeka I:* Supreme Court rules racial segregation in public is unconstitutional.

May 31—
Brown v. *Board of Education of Topeka II:* Supreme Court says desegregation of public schools must proceed "with all deliberate speed."

August 28—
14-year-old Emmett Till is killed in Money, Mississippi.

December 5, 1955–December 20, 1956—
Montgomery, Alabama bus boycott.

November 13—
Supreme Court outlaws racial segregation on Alabama's city buses.

January 10, 11—
Southern Christian Leadership Conference (SCLC) is founded.

August 29—
Civil Rights Act is passed. Among other things, it creates Civil Rights Commission to advise the president and gives government power to uphold voting rights.

September 1957–
Little Rock Central High School is desegregated.

—1962— —1963— —1964—

September 29—
Federal troops help integrate University of Mississippi ("Ole Miss") after two people are killed and several are injured.

April to May—
Birmingham, Alabama, demonstrations. School children join the marches.

May 20—
Supreme Court rules Birmingham's segregation laws are unconstitutional.

June 12—
NAACP worker Medgar Evers is killed in Jackson, Mississippi.

August 28—
March on Washington draws more than 250,000 people.

September 15—
Four girls are killed when a Birmingham church is bombed.

November 22—
President John F. Kennedy is killed in Dallas, Texas.

March–June—
St. Augustine, Florida, demonstrations.

June 21—
James Chaney, Michael Schwerner, and Andrew Goodman are killed while registering black voters in Mississippi.

July 2—
Civil Rights Act is passed. Among other things, it provides for equal job opportunities and gives the government power to sue to desegregate public schools and facilities.

August—
Mississippi Freedom Democratic Party (MFDP) attempts to represent Mississippi at the Democratic National Convention.

2

—1958————1959————1960————1961—

September 1958–August 1959—
Little Rock Central High School is closed because governor refuses to integrate it.

February 1—
Student sit-ins at lunch counter in Greensboro, North Carolina, begin sit-in protests all over the South.

April 17—
Student Nonviolent Coordinating Committee (SNCC) is founded.

May 6—
Civil Rights Act is passed. Among other things, it allows judges to appoint people to help blacks register to vote.

Eleven African countries win their independence.

May 4—
Freedom Rides leave Washington, D.C., and head south.

September 22—
Interstate Commerce Commission ordered to enforce desegregation laws on buses, and trains, and in travel facilities like waiting rooms, rest rooms, and restaurants.

—1965————1966————1967————1968—

January–March—
Selma, Alabama, demonstrations.

February 21—
Malcolm X is killed in New York City.

March 21–25—
More than 25,000 march from Selma to Montgomery, Alabama.

August 6—
Voting Rights Act passed.

August 11–16—
Watts riot (Los Angeles, California).

June—
James Meredith "March Against Fear" from Memphis, Tennessee, to Jackson, Mississippi. Stokely Carmichael makes slogan "Black Power" famous during march.

Fall—
Black Panther Party for Self-Defense is formed by Huey Newton and Bobby Seale in Oakland, California.

June 13—
Thurgood Marshall is appointed first African-American U.S. Supreme Court justice.

Summer—
Riots break out in 30 U.S. cities.

April 4—
Martin Luther King, Jr., is killed in Memphis, Tennessee.

April 11—
Civil Rights Act is passed. Among other things, it prohibits discrimination in selling and renting houses or apartments.

May 13–June 23—
Poor People's March: Washington, D.C., to protest poverty.

CIVIL RIGHTS MOVEMENT TIME LINE   **3**

1 A BURNING HOUSE

> *All our lives we have been taught that we are the inferior. When we were little and the white boys and the colored were going to play cowboys and Indians, who was Tom Mix and Buck Jones or the Lone Ranger? The Whites. Who were we? Tonto, his flunky. If we were going to play shipwrecked, who was Robinson Crusoe? The Whites. Who was man Friday? Guess who.*

MALCOLM X , from an FBI report on a speech he gave to his New York City temple in 1957

"I remember being suddenly snatched awake into a frightening confusion of pistol shots and shouting and smoke and flames. My father had shouted and shot at the

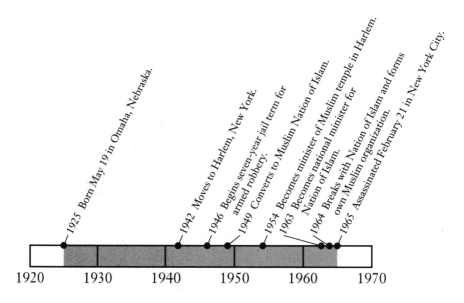

1925 Born May 19 in Omaha, Nebraska.
1942 Moves to Harlem, New York.
1946 Begins seven-year jail term for armed robbery.
1949 Converts to Muslim Nation of Islam.
1954 Becomes minister of Muslim temple in Harlem.
1963 Becomes national minister for Nation of Islam.
1964 Breaks with Nation of Islam and forms own Muslim organization.
1965 Assassinated February 21 in New York City.

1920   1930   1940   1950   1960   1970

two white men who had set [the] fire and were running away. Our home was burning down around us. We were lunging and bumping and tumbling all over each other trying to escape. My mother, with the baby in her arms, just made it into the yard before the house crashed in, showering sparks. I remember we were outside in the night in our underwear, crying and yelling our heads off. The white police and firemen came and stood around as the house burned down to the ground."

Malcolm Little (we know him as both Malcolm X and El Hajj Malik El Shabazz) was only four years old when his home was burned to the ground. It was no accident. Two people had come to the house in the middle of the night and had thrown burning torches through the windows. They didn't want the Little family to live in their neighborhood. They thought they could scare the family off by destroying their home.

Malcolm's family didn't know who had set fire to their home. His family probably had never met these people. They certainly hadn't done anything bad to make these people angry with them. But they did know this: The two men with torches were white, and the Little family was black. If they had been the same color, it would never have happened.

Malcolm was too young to understand why some whites hated blacks. He was too young to understand that some people get frightened by others just because they're different. He was too young to understand how fear becomes hate. But that little boy who stood there, shivering and crying in the winter night, with his face lit up by the orange glow of the fire, would one day fight that hate as no one had ever done before.

Malcolm X's story is about drugs, stealing, gambling, and guns. It's about prison, pride, power, and hope. It's about love and peace, hatred and violence. It's about God and strength, the devil and weakness, Africa and Asia, Harlem and Mississippi. It's about a new life, and a death that had no meaning. It's about a man who died while trying to set his own people free.

Some people have always known who Malcolm X was and what he stood for. Others have never understood him because he was so many things. Malcolm was always growing and changing. He was always building new lives for himself, just like houses. Some of these houses were burned down. Others simply weren't big enough for what Malcolm needed. So he left them and moved on. But if Malcolm created many different houses in his life, they were always built on the same things: anger about the way his people had been treated, the courage to talk about it, and the vision of freedom to lead and guide him.

That cold night back in 1929 had frightened Malcolm. But it came as no surprise to his mother and father. The Reverend Earl Little and his wife, Louise Little, had been through this sort of thing before. The last time was just before Malcolm was born. They were living in Omaha, Nebraska, and Rev. Earl Little was away from home. Some people riding horses with hoods covering their faces had galloped around the house smashing all the windows. Before they left, they had warned Mrs. Little to take her family out of town. They also told her to stop her husband from preaching among the "good Negroes" of Omaha.

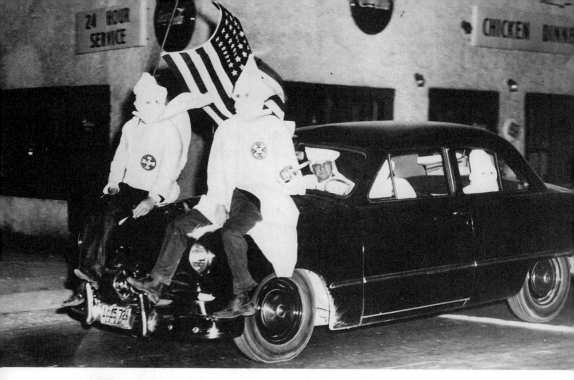

Members of the KKK traveled openly throughout the South, confronting African Americans with terror.

Malcolm's father was a powerful-looking man—he was more than six feet tall. He was a Baptist minister who preached about freedom for black people and the rights of black people. He talked about a black nation that would rise up in North America. He jumped and shouted in the pulpit—not just to spread the word of Jesus but also to spread the word of black pride. Rev. Earl Little felt it was time African Americans remembered that they were a great people. Many words have been used in the United States to describe blacks, or African Americans. Depending upon how a word was used, it could be insulting or reflect pride. These words include *Negro, colored,* and *people of color*—as well as *black* and *African American.*

Slavery had caused many whites to think that blacks were like a sack of potatoes that could be sold and traded, and made to work for next to nothing. In 1865, slavery was made illegal in the part of the U.S. Constitution called the 13th Amendment. Even so, everyday life for black people didn't change much. As far as Rev. Earl Little was concerned, most African Americans were still being treated as if they were slaves. He wanted to change this.

Many whites liked the way things were. Blacks worked hard for them, and they did so for very little money. They were used to treating African Americans as if they were inferior people. It would be difficult to change white people's traditions and customs. It would be difficult to force them to accept African Americans as the human beings they were. Whites not only liked the way things were, they had thought up an entire system of rules to keep it that way. In the South, many of these rules were written down as city laws or laws of the state. These rules were known as the Jim Crow laws. They kept whites and blacks separated, or segregated. They helped to nourish the prejudice against African Americans—the idea that blacks aren't as good as whites and should be treated differently. Blacks had to tip their hats to whites and call them "sir" and "ma'am" no matter how old they were. Even if a black man was 60 years old, he still had to call a white teenager "sir." This made many African Americans angry. Every day a poison dripped into young black minds—a poison that gave black children a painful feeling that they weren't as good as white children.

In the North, segregation was also a way of life. Unlike the South, though, this wasn't a law that had been written down somewhere. It was just the custom or tradition.

In 1896, the Supreme Court only made things worse. In a case called *Plessy* v. *Ferguson*, the Court said that as long as schools, restaurants, or hospitals were "equal" it was legal to separate whites and blacks. But these places were never equal. In their classrooms black children often went without textbooks, or the books they had were old or were missing pages. Schools for black children often had no heat or indoor toilets, and sometimes no chalkboards. Much more money was spent on schools for whites than on those for blacks. As a result, teachers found it difficult to give black children the same quality of education whites received.

Most blacks did not have the courage to challenge the way things were. They couldn't. If they complained, they might be shot or killed by whites, or chased out of town. For them survival was more important than freedom. But for Malcolm's father, freedom and survival were the same thing.

After their house was burned down in Lansing, Michigan, the Little family moved twice and ended up in the country just outside of East Lansing, where Rev. Earl Little built a four-room house.

Malcolm was his father's seventh child. Rev. Earl Little had been married to someone else before he married Louise. He and his first wife had lived in Boston, Massachusetts, where they had three children: Ella, Earl, and Mary. But Earl had separated from his first wife and moved to Philadelphia with the children. There he met and married Louise. By the time he had built the house in Lansing, Mrs. Little had borne Rev. Earl Little six more children: Wilfred, Hilda, Philbert, Malcolm, Reginald, and Yvonne. Two more children would soon follow: Wesley and Robert.

Malcolm had the lightest skin of all the children. He got his reddish-brown skin and hair color from his mother. She was so light that some white people didn't know she was an African American. Malcolm's mother felt ashamed of her light skin. Her mother had been raped by a white man on the island of Grenada, her home. He wasn't interested in accepting his responsibilities as a father. He deserted the daughter that was born. It always seemed to Malcolm that his mother took this out on him, telling him to get some sun, or beating him harder than she did the others. It seemed that he reminded her of the man who had raped her mother.

Malcolm's father wasn't like his mother. He always seemed to have a soft spot for Malcolm. Malcolm never knew why this was. Maybe, he thought later, it was because even his father couldn't help believing that lighter is better. Rev. Earl Little beat all of his sons except Malcolm, who got all of his punishment from his mother.

In many ways, the life the Little family had in Michigan was a good one. They grew food, raised chickens, and made their own clothes. They saved the money that Rev. Earl Little made from his preaching to open a store. Malcolm spent his free time hunting and shooting rabbits or tending his own vegetable garden. He loved to lie on a grassy hill all afternoon, gazing up at the clouds and thinking "all kinds of things," as he later said.

As Malcolm grew older, his father took him to some of the secret meetings he attended—meetings where people talked about black pride and freedom. Rev. Earl Little never took any

of his other children to these meetings, just Malcolm. Hidden safely behind locked doors and covered windows, Malcolm watched people listen as his father talked. Then he heard those magic words—Marcus Garvey.

During the 1920s, Marcus Garvey had become one of the most talked-about black men in America. He inspired black people everywhere with a new sense of pride in their race and a vision that one day they would return to the homeland of their ancestors—Africa. Garvey, who was from Jamaica, tried to persuade the African people in America to try to build a black nation. This was a dream that both Rev. Earl Little and his son Malcolm shared.

"I asked," Garvey once wrote, "'where is the black man's Government...? where is his King, and his kingdom...? Where is his President, his country, and his ambassador, his army, his navy, his men of big affairs?' I could not find them, and then I declared, 'I will help to make them.'"

Garvey had people all over the country working for him and organizing local branches of his movement. Malcolm's father was one of these people. Some of the whites knew this, and that's why they burned down the family's house.

Suddenly, one night in 1931, Malcolm woke up to the sound of his mother's screams. All the children scrambled out of bed and into the living room, where the police were trying to calm Mrs. Little. Malcolm was only six, but he would never forget that moment. "And all of us children who were staring knew without anyone having to say it that something terrible had happened to our father," he said.

Rev. Earl Little had been found lying across the streetcar tracks. His body had been cut almost in half, and one side of his skull had been smashed in. No one ever found out what really happened, but there was no doubt that he had been murdered. The blacks in Lansing knew that the whites were responsible. They knew the whites were frightened of what he was saying.

If his father had lived, Malcolm might have walked in his

Back-to-Africa movement leader Marcus Garvey, shown before his deportation back to Jamaica.

footsteps and taken to the pulpit. But his father was snatched away from him, and only the seeds of Rev. Earl Little's teachings remained with his son. These seeds would not grow for many years to come. In the meantime, for Malcolm another house had suddenly burned down around him. His father, that great and wonderful tower of strength, was gone.

WELFARE BOY

> ❝ *They didn't even have any Negro firemen when I was a youth. When I was a youth, the only thing you could dream about becoming was a good waiter or a good busboy or a good shoeshine man. I mean that's the American dream. Back when I was a youth, that's the way it was, and I didn't grow up in Mississippi either—I grew up in Michigan ... It was then that I began to change—inside... I drew away from white people... Where 'nigger' had slipped off my back before, wherever I heard it now, I stopped and looked at whoever said it.* ❞

MALCOLM X (age 15)

With Earl Little's death, things began to change for the Little family. They had two insurance policies, but only one company paid what was due. The other company claimed that Rev. Earl Little had committed suicide and refused to honor the policy. They managed to live on the insurance money for a while, but it wasn't enough to keep the family fed and clothed for long. Wilfred realized that his mother couldn't care for all of them on her own, so he left school to help her. He found work wherever he could. Hilda also left school to look after the babies while her mother and Wilfred worked in town.

Mrs. Little struggled to take care of her family. Like her husband, she was extremely proud and found it difficult to accept any form of charity. But there were eight hungry mouths to feed, and she had to do something. America was in the middle of a terrible slump called the Great Depression, which lasted all through the 1930s. Work was difficult to find, and even food was scarce at times if you were poor. Mrs. Little had no choice but to accept help wherever she could find it. Like other poor people, she turned to the welfare department. This is a service offered by the state that provides the poor with enough clothes and food to survive. In return for the small amount of money they received, however, the Little family had to give up their privacy. Officers from the welfare department came by when they weren't invited. They constantly checked on the family, snooping around the house and suggesting to the children behind their mother's back that she wasn't able to look after them properly.

By 1934, the family began to suffer even more. Malcolm and Philbert often walked the two miles to town with a nickel to buy a bag of stale bread. Malcolm remembered: " . . . there were times when there wasn't even a nickel and we would be so hungry we were dizzy. My mother would boil a big pot of dandelion greens, and we would eat that." He and his brothers shot rabbits, trapped muskrats, and caught bullfrogs. They would eat some of this and sell the rest to the whites up the road who weren't much better off than they were. After a while, though, Mrs. Little had to ask for free food from the state. The

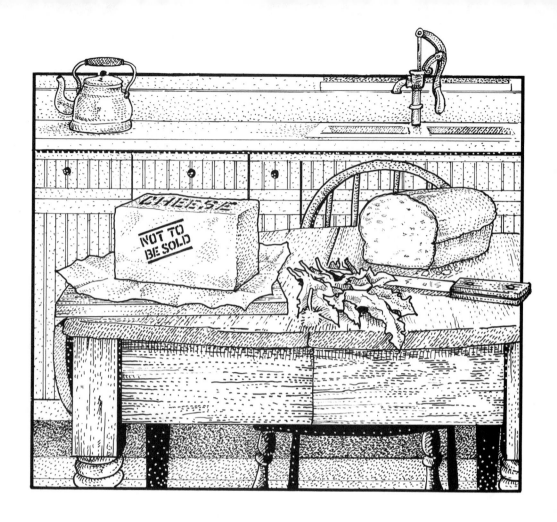

family felt ashamed, but it was the only way they could live. The checks from the state weren't enough, and there was very little work for African Americans.

The welfare people came around more and more. Louise was finding the strain difficult to bear. She began to talk to herself and to withdraw into her own world. Malcolm often went to friends' homes at dinnertime, knowing that he would be invited to stay and eat. He also stole fruit from some of the grocery stores in town. After he had been caught a few times, the welfare people decided that it was time they did something about the Little family. They thought Malcolm caused more trouble than any of the others, so they forced Mrs. Little to give him up. He was sent to live with some neighbors, the Gohannas family. This was the beginning of the end of the Little family. Before long, Malcolm's mother suffered a complete nervous breakdown. She was taken to the State Mental Hospital in Kalamazoo, Michigan. All the other children, except Wilfred and Hilda, the oldest, were sent to live with other African-American families in the area.

Malcolm never forgave the welfare people for breaking up his family. He felt guilty that he hadn't done more to stop it. He believed that if the welfare people had only left them alone, they would have survived. Whites had murdered his father, and now they had taken away his mother and put her into a hospital where she would remain for 26 years. It was as if another house had burned down for Malcolm. His family was gone.

Malcolm was a strong boy, and he decided to make the best of what he had. He liked his new family, and they treated him well. At least now he had enough food and proper clothes for the first time in a long while.

He was now 12 years old. It was a time for school and homework, as well as games, pranks, and rabbit hunting. But one prank got Malcolm into more trouble than he could ever have imagined: He turned up in class wearing a hat.

Wearing hats was against school rules. As punishment, Malcolm was ordered to walk around and around the classroom. But he was determined to have the last laugh. On one trip past the teacher's chair, he carefully placed a thumbtack in the seat. It worked! The teacher was furious, and the whole class burst out laughing. But Malcolm was expelled for his little joke. He didn't mind. That happened when he was only 13. Being expelled just meant that he would have lots of free time. The welfare people had other plans, however. They sent him to a children's prison called a reform school.

Malcolm didn't go directly to reform school. First he went to a kind of halfway house called a detention home. It was like a test. If he behaved, he could stay. If he didn't, he would have to go on to the children's prison. The detention home was in

Mason, Michigan, 12 miles from Lansing. It didn't seem too bad. He liked the white people who ran the home, Mr. and Mrs. Swerlin, and they liked him. For the very first time in his life, Malcolm had his own room. He worked hard at the chores he shared with all the other boys and girls—and he tried harder than ever to gain the respect of this new family. The Swerlins saw how well Malcolm was doing. He must have passed the test. He stayed in the detention home, but almost everyone else went on to the reform school. He knew that Mr. and Mrs. Swerlin were keeping him, and he was grateful. He didn't want to leave.

When Mrs. Swerlin arranged for Malcolm to go to Mason Junior High, the only school in town, he entered the seventh grade. There was only one other black family in Mason, the Lyons, and some of their children were in the lower grades. All of Malcolm's other schoolmates were white, but this didn't bother him. He made friends quickly and joined all sorts of school clubs and societies. He became a member of the school's basketball team. He also got a job washing dishes in town and managed to save enough money to buy himself a green suit and some shoes for the times when he went to Lansing on weekends to visit his brothers and sisters.

By the second half of the school year, Malcolm was elected class president. Mrs. Swerlin was pleased that he was doing so well. His grades were among the highest in the school. Most important of all, Malcolm was happy. But there would soon be another change in Malcolm's life. Ella, his half sister from Boston, came to visit the family.

"I think the major impact of Ella's arrival, at least upon me, was that she was the first really proud black woman I had ever seen in my life. She was plainly proud of her very dark skin. This was unheard of among Negroes in those days, especially in Lansing," Malcolm remembered.

Ella brought the family back together for a little while. She took all of her brothers and sisters to see their mother at the hospital. She told them about all the other Littles in Georgia and Boston. "We Littles have to stick together," she said. But she disappeared as fast as she had come—back to Boston, to her second husband, and to a world Malcolm could only dream of. She had taken a liking to the tall, confident 15-year-old, however, and told him to write to her regularly. Much to Malcolm's delight, she also invited him to visit. He couldn't wait. As soon as the summer of 1940 arrived, he was on a Greyhound bus bound for Boston.

Malcolm never forgot that first trip to Boston. It was one of the most important things he ever decided to do. It didn't last long, though. Before he could believe it, he was back home in Mason. But he couldn't forget the sights and sounds of the big city: the neon lights, the expensive cars, busy streets, fancy stores, and crowded nightclubs. He had never seen so many people! Most important, he had never seen so many black people.

Boston and Ella had had a strong effect on Malcolm. He had seen how other African Americans lived in a big city. Now he looked at where he lived. He looked at his school, which was nearly all white. He began to listen more carefully to what people said around him. Ella and her friends would never allow themselves to be called "nigger." But the Swerlins used that word over a hundred times a day. Malcolm didn't like the way he was being treated. "It just never dawned upon them that I could understand, that I wasn't a pet, but a human being," he said. "They didn't give me credit for having the same sensitivity, intellect, and understanding that they would have been ready and willing to recognize in a white boy in my position.... Even though they appeared to have opened the door, it was still closed. Thus, they never did really see *me*.... I learned things I never forgot."

In school it was the same. Malcolm was the only African American in his class. He realized that the only reason he was so popular was because he was a "mascot"—a black boy who fit perfectly into a white world. "I was unique in my class, like a pink poodle," he said. "And I was proud; I'm not going to say I wasn't. In fact, by then, I didn't really have much feeling about being a Negro, because I was trying so hard, in every way I could to be white."

Malcolm was also discovering who he was, and he was proud of the fact that he was different—that he was an African American. Ella had taught him that. Now, on the basketball team when they visited other schools, words like "coon," "rastus," or "nigger" that had never really bothered Malcolm before shot into him like arrows. One experience, however, made him more angry than anything else.

According to Malcolm, here's what happened: One afternoon English class had finished and Malcolm found himself alone with the teacher, Mr. Ostrowski, whom he both liked and admired. Mr. Ostrowski was a "natural-born advisor," always telling the class to follow their dreams, even if these dreams didn't seem practical or possible. Mr. Ostrowski asked Malcolm whether he had considered a career. Malcolm answered with the first thing that came to mind.

"Well, yes, sir, I've been thinking I'd like to be a lawyer."

Malcolm couldn't believe what Mr. Ostrowski said.

"Malcolm, one of the first needs is for us to be realistic. Don't misunderstand me, now. We all like you here, you know that. But you've got to be realistic about being a nigger. A lawyer—that's no realistic goal for a nigger."

He had been insulted many times before, but it never seemed as painful as this. Malcolm realized that he could never be part of the white world as a real person, only as the person they wanted him to be. He started spending more and more time on his own. Everyone noticed the change in him, but Malcolm wouldn't say anything. He knew that Ella was the only person who would understand him.

Ella did understand. She made arrangements with the welfare people to take care of Malcolm herself. As soon as eighth

grade was finished, he was back on the bus on his way to Boston. This time it was for good.

Later, Malcolm thought about that time in his life. He decided that no move in his life had ever affected him as deeply as this move to Boston. Malcolm's real journey was just beginning.

3 A COUNTRY CAT

> *Shorty would take me to groovy, frantic scenes in different chicks' and cats' pads, where with the lights and juke down mellow, everybody... jumped. I met chicks who were fine as May wine, and cats who were hip to all happenings.*

MALCOLM X (Boston)

Ella told Malcolm to do two things: discover the city before looking for a job and always lock the front door. Malcolm wasted no time. He was off into the heart of Boston before Ella knew it. This time Malcolm wanted to see all of Boston—not just the Sugar Hill section of Roxbury, where Ella lived. He spent every day wandering down the narrow cobbled streets of old Boston. He hung around the docks of Boston Harbor and tried to imagine crates of tea being dumped from the tall ships that had docked there almost 200 years ago. He lost himself in the crowds at the bus and railway stations.

He couldn't wait to have enough money to watch movies in the air-conditioned theaters and go to one of the big ballrooms to hear some of his favorite bands play.

As time went on, Malcolm found himself drawn like a magnet to the poorer sections of Boston. "That world of grocery stores, walk-up flats, cheap restaurants, poolrooms, bars, storefront churches, and pawnshops seemed to hold a natural lure for me," he admitted. Malcolm felt more at home in this part of Roxbury than in Ella's more well-to-do neighborhood. "Not only was this part of Roxbury much more exciting, but I felt more relaxed among Negroes who were being their natural selves and not putting on airs," he said.

Malcolm envied the slick young people, or "cats," who hung out on the street corners outside pool halls. He noticed their expensive clothes and smooth hair, which they had made straight with special chemicals. He watched them smoke, drink, and gamble. He learned how to talk the way they talked; he learned their slang. Life here was so different from life in Mason and Lansing. He found it difficult to put all the wonder and excitement into words when he wrote to his brothers and sisters.

Malcolm had made friends with a boy called "Shorty," who worked in one of the pool halls racking up the balls. They found out that they were both from Lansing. Then Shorty took charge of Malcolm and promised to teach him all he needed to know. By the next day, Shorty had already lined up a job for Malcolm. He was going to be the new shoeshine boy at a big dance and music hall called the Roseland State Ballroom. Ella wasn't impressed. She didn't like the idea of Malcolm's hanging out with people like these. But she couldn't do anything about it—Malcolm was determined.

"The main thing you got to remember is that everything in the world is a hustle. So long, Red," said Freddie, the old shoeshine boy, when he had finished showing Malcolm what to do. Freddie had told Malcolm how to make extra tips by handing out towels, brushing down men's suits, replacing shoelaces, and even supplying some of the men with the telephone numbers of women who would go out with them.

"*Crack*" went Malcolm's rag like a Chinese firecracker as he finished polishing musician Duke Ellington's shoes. Malcolm was so proud of the fact that he was working where some of the world's most famous musicians played—and shining their shoes, too. When there was no one waiting for a shoeshine, Malcolm liked to slip downstairs and peer into the huge room. There he would watch a sea of people dancing and laughing. How he wished he could join them! He had never seen such dancing back home. The craze in those days was a step called the lindy hop. It was a fast dance in which men and women threw themselves wildly into the air and through each other's arms and legs.

In Boston, Malcolm threw himself into the life of the city with more energy than he had ever done anything. He didn't avoid its bad parts either. He began smoking marijuana, or pot, drinking a lot, and even gambling a little with Shorty and his friends. He bought his first zoot suit with Shorty. Zoot suits had big balloonlike pants that became very narrow at the ankles and a long coat that reached down to the knees. Shorty even made Malcolm's hair straight by "conking" it with a mixture of ingredients that burned Malcolm's scalp. He stood in the mirror looking at himself in his wild suit and straight hair. He thought he was the coolest kid in town. But his memories of that first conk would change later in his life:

"This was my first really big step toward self-degradation [dragging myself down]: when I endured all of that pain, literally burning my flesh to have it look like a white man's hair. I had joined that multitude [large number] of Negro men and women in America who are brainwashed into believing that the black people are 'inferior'—and white people 'superior'—that they will even violate and mutilate [try to change] their God-created bodies to try to look 'pretty' by white standards."

Malcolm now felt that having shed his country clothes and habits, he had become one of Boston's slick cats. He was still only 16, but he was tall and strong-looking. He looked much older than he really was. It was time to move on. Cool cats don't shine shoes. Malcolm quit his job at the ballroom, and Ella persuaded him to take a job serving behind the counter of a nearby drugstore. Ella was happy that he now had a good job in a good neighborhood. Malcolm was happy because the job gave him some extra money to spend. More important, it gave him the nights to go lindy-hopping. He became a good dancer, often stealing the spotlight as he and his partner danced alone out on the floor.

Malcolm started going out with a girl named Laura. This didn't last long, and soon he was dating another girl named Sophia. Sophia was white. Many of his friends looked up to him for this. They thought it was cool to have a white girlfriend. Ella, who had adored Laura, now treated Malcolm like a snake. She didn't like the idea of his seeing a white girl. As a result, Malcolm moved out of Ella's house. He went to live with Shorty and began a new job as a busboy (a boy who cleans up tables after people have eaten) at the Parker House Hotel.

"Sorry, I'm late," shouted Malcolm as he arrived very late to work one Sunday morning. But no one seemed to notice. The world was buzzing with more important news. A few hours earlier, Japanese pilots had bombed the American fleet in Pearl Harbor. This was December 7, 1941. The United States jumped into World War II to help its friends around the world and to defend itself. Who could have known how this would change things back in Roxbury?

As 1942 rolled around, tens of thousands of young American men were marching off to war. This meant that there weren't enough men and women to fill all the jobs at home. For Malcolm, this was perfect. He was too young to join the army, but he looked old enough to get any job he wanted. "Yes, I'm over

Young Malcolm in his zoot suit before discovering the Nation of Islam.

21," lied Malcolm when he went to sign on at the railroad. In fact, he was still only 17.

It was Ella who had suggested the railroad to Malcolm. She was eager to get him out of Boston and away from Sophia, his white girlfriend. She also felt that some travel might bring him to his senses and give him a chance to meet new friends. Malcolm liked the idea for different reasons. Sure, as a fourth cook he would have to wander up and down the train selling coffee and snacks, make sure the kitchen had enough food, and wash the dirty dishes. He didn't mind. The important thing for

Harlem Night Life

In the early 1900s, Harlem became a nearly all-black section of New York City. During the 1920s Harlem was the center of a great cultural and intellectual movement among African-American writers, artists, and musicians. It was called the New Negro Movement and sometimes the Harlem Renaissance. Night clubs, such as the Cotton Club, were popular night spots for jazz, a new American music created by black musicians. Cab Calloway and Louis Armstrong were two popular musicians then.

By the time Malcolm X arrived in Harlem, the Renaissance was no longer in its heyday. But Harlem's nightlife was still "jumping" with singers such as Billie Holiday, and the big bands of Count Basie and Duke Ellington.

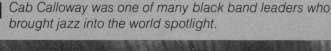

Cab Calloway was one of many black band leaders who brought jazz into the world spotlight.

Harlem's famed Cotton Club, for many years a great showcase for black performers, in 1930.

Billie Holiday, one of the greatest blues singers ever, helped bring jazz to a growing audience.

Malcolm was that in those days the trains were the heartbeat of the nation. They rattled from one city to the next, linking the booming towns of the United States like the veins of a body. It was his chance to explore other cities. And of all the cities Malcolm passed through, there was one that he wanted to go to more than any of the others: the biggest and brightest city of all—New York City.

Though he started out on The Colonial, which ran from Boston to Washington, D.C., Malcolm later got a transfer that allowed him to replace the sandwich man on the Yankee Clipper. This train ran from Boston to New York. The day the train pulled into New York City, Malcolm was into his zoot suit before the first passenger had gotten off. He had heard all about New York. He had heard of Broadway and Times Square. And, of course, Harlem. Malcolm couldn't wait to have his first taste of the big city.

Malcolm's visits to Harlem were like a magic spell. From a comfortable neighborhood of Boston's black section, he arrived in New York to stay "in the slum blocks of old rat-trap apartment houses, just crawling with everything you could mention that was illegal and immoral." Malcolm had been drawn to the poor area of Boston, and now Harlem's dirty streets excited him even more. He lived on the excitement of Harlem's nights. This was his world, and it was bigger and "badder" than anywhere he had ever been.

Harlemites, or people who lived in Harlem, began to recognize Malcolm. He began to make friends among the musicians of Harlem. Back in Roxbury, he used to party all night with Sophia on his arm and then go to work. He was almost always high on some kind of drug, whether it was drink or pot or both. In Harlem, with his growing number of friends, he began to stay out all night. He would get only a few hours of sleep in a boardinghouse before it was time to go back to Boston.

It didn't last. Malcolm knew that he would lose his job sooner or later. He used such foul language that the older cooks and waiters had made bets about how long "Sandwich Red," as they called him, would be around. When he was fired, he decided to visit his family back in Lansing. They hardly recognized him. Dressed in a wild zoot suit, with orange conked hair, a hat with a wide brim, and dazzling shoes, he seemed like something from another planet. He visited his mother in the hospital. She only just recognized her son. Malcolm loved to impress everybody with his new life, but he couldn't wait to get back to the city.

For a while, Malcolm had another railroad job on the Silver Meteor to St. Petersburg and Miami, Florida. But he soon got in trouble with one of the conductors there and found himself back in New York, with no money at all. By this time, Malcolm had begun to feel more at home in New York than he did in Boston. It was time to put down some roots, to make his mark, and dive into the world Harlem offered. The very same day he had been fired from the Silver Meteor, he was offered a job as a waiter in the famous nightclub Small's Paradise. It seemed like the right time to build himself another house—this time in Harlem.

THE HARLEM HUSTLE

> **When you become an animal, a vulture, in the ghetto, as I had become, you enter a world of animals and vultures. It becomes truly the survival of only the fittest.**
>
> **MALCOLM X (Harlem)**

The customers at Small's Paradise liked the way Malcolm worked. He was fast and efficient, polite and helpful. They often shared their adventures with Malcolm. They told him about some of the most daring crimes that ever took place. Some of them were small-time gangsters themselves. They taught him how to recognize a policeman when he saw one. They taught him where to find drugs, where to sell stolen goods, and how to rob a house. They started calling him "Detroit Red." Malcolm had told them that he came from Detroit because he thought no one had ever heard of Lansing.

Malcolm worked hard and played hard. He gambled away most of the money he made on the "numbers." This was an illegal betting game that many people in Harlem played. You had to guess numbers such as how many shares would be bought and sold on the stock market that day. At other times he went to the movie houses, listened to bands play, or "hung out" smoking pot with his friends.

In the early hours of the morning, just before dawn, Malcolm used to collapse on his bed in a boardinghouse on St. Nicholas Avenue. He was exhausted by the loose and reckless kind of life he was leading. Most of the rooms at the boardinghouse were taken by women who were prostitutes or drug addicts. Malcolm found these women fascinating. "It was in this house that I learned more about women than I ever did in any other single place," he said.

One afternoon, in early 1943, things were slow at Small's Paradise. Malcolm noticed a soldier sitting alone at one of his tables. "He looked dumb and pitiful and just up from the Deep South," Malcolm remembered. Malcolm served the soldier four or five drinks. Then he strolled over and asked if he would like a woman (Malcolm really meant a prostitute). The man looked up and smiled. "That would be nice," he said. Malcolm scribbled down the address of one of his prostitute friends at the boardinghouse, and the man disappeared.

Now there were some things that waiters never did at Small's Paradise. They weren't supposed to sell drugs or stolen goods or to find prostitutes for men in the army or navy. This could get the restaurant closed down by the army or navy police within minutes. Malcolm, however, thought he could smell out an army or navy spy if he saw one. This guy just didn't look like one of them. He could not have been more wrong. The soldier was one of the army spies. As soon as Malcolm gave him the address, the man went straight to the police.

At the police station they shouted and threatened to send him to jail, but he was "clean." He had never been in trouble with the police before, so they just frightened him and then let him go. Malcolm's real punishment came from Charlie Small, the owner of Small's Paradise. Malcolm wasn't just fired, he wasn't allowed to enter the nightclub again. This was a heavy blow to Malcolm. Small's had become his home. Now Malcolm turned to the only friend he could trust, Sammy the Pimp.

Sammy was a thin, well-dressed man who made his money by organizing a small group of prostitutes. That's how he got his name. Sammy suggested that for Malcolm the easiest hustle (this is a quick way of making money often by trickery or illegal means) was selling pot. He told Malcolm where to get his supply of marijuana and lent him $20 to get started. That night Malcolm returned. He gave Sammy the $20 back and even offered to lend *him* some. Malcolm had made a profit in just one day! It was an easy hustle for Malcolm. All of his musician friends smoked reefers (cigarettes stuffed with pot), and they all knew and trusted "Detroit Red." Malcolm was in business.

"I kept turning over my profit, increasing my supplies, and I sold reefers like a wild man," explained Malcolm. "I scarcely slept; I was wherever musicians [got together]. A roll of money was in my pocket. Every day, I cleared at least fifty or sixty dollars. In those days ... this was a fortune to a seventeen-year-old Negro. I felt, for the first time in my life, that great feeling of *free*! Suddenly, now, I was the peer of the other young hustlers I had admired."

Malcolm knew that he was entering a dangerous world. He began to carry a small gun pressed under his belt in the small of his back—somewhere the police didn't usually look in a body search. He started to move a lot. That way, the police couldn't hide anything in his room when he was out. They often did this to frame people. In other words, they broke into people's apartments and pretended to discover drugs that they themselves had hidden earlier.

Selling the pot became more and more risky. The police knew he was selling, and they were after him. Malcolm sold fewer and fewer reefers because he had to be so careful. Sammy came up with another clever idea for Malcolm. He saw that things were getting dangerous for Malcolm there in Harlem. He suggested that Malcolm use his old railroad papers to travel all over the country. This way he could sell reefers to his musician friends who were on tour with their bands. No one had ever heard of a traveling reefer salesman, but it worked. Malcolm had no trouble getting free rides on the trains, and he knew enough musicians to travel from one place to the next selling his reefers. When his supply ran out, he'd return to New York, stock up, and then head for wherever another band was playing.

One day, Malcolm received a greeting from Uncle Sam. He was being drafted, or called to fight in the army—World War II. Malcolm had no intention of leaving Harlem. But it wasn't easy to escape from the draft. He decided to pretend he was crazy. He ranted and raved about the army, about how he wanted to go down south and fight there, where there was no war at all! His trick worked. He knew that the army had spies in Harlem. By the time he had to go for his examination, army officials had heard all about this crazy Malcolm Little. He wore his most unusual zoot suit and orange shoes, and spoke in the thickest slang any of those people had ever heard. "... I want to get down south. Organize them nigger soldiers, you dig? Steal us some guns, and kill up crackers [white southerners]!" he told the doctor who interviewed him. The army rejected him.

Malcolm began to drift further into the criminal life of Harlem. He was tired of traveling on the trains, and he was unable to sell enough reefers to make a living. He turned to stealing instead. With Sammy, he traveled to nearby cities to steal. During this time he took cocaine, a far more dangerous drug than marijuana. He started carrying bigger guns and moving from place to place, never staying anywhere for long.

When his younger brother Reginald decided to live with him, Malcolm slowed down a little. They found an apartment together, and Malcolm started to work in the numbers business as

a "runner." This meant that he would carry the money and betting slips from the players to the dealers. Then he took 10 percent of all the money that people had bet.

On some nights Malcolm waited on the corner of 45th Street and Broadway. He wore a suit and a white flower in his lapel. This was called "steering." Customers had been told to look for Malcolm. He would then "steer," or bring, them up to Harlem to meet whatever kind of women they wanted to meet. He was amazed by how important and rich some of his clients were. Among them were "society leaders ... big politicians ... tycoons ... celebrities...."

Despite his different money-making schemes, life became more and more difficult for Malcolm. He was now addicted to drugs, and he gambled all of his money on the numbers. When another red-headed African American stuck up a bar, Malcolm ran away to Michigan. He was afraid some people might think he had done it. Malcolm returned only after another "red" confessed.

Malcolm gave up "steering" and began smuggling illegal, or "bootleg," alcohol into Harlem from Long Island. Things went from bad to worse. Once again, another "red" had held up a business and Malcolm was a suspect. Worse than this, Malcolm got into an argument with the one person he shouldn't have argued with—West Indian Archie.

West Indian Archie was an old-time hustler who was one of those "real bad Negroes." If you crossed him, he wouldn't think twice about killing you. West Indian Archie ran the numbers. He took people's bets and paid them if they "hit" the right numbers. Malcolm thought he had hit, and he claimed $300 from Archie. Archie paid, but he later checked his list and found that Malcolm was wrong. Word began to spread that Archie was very upset. Malcolm was scared, but he couldn't run. He would have lost everyone's respect. He went to hear Billie Holliday—one of his friends—sing. Even she could sense that something was wrong with "Detroit Red" that night. Malcolm stayed up smoking reefers, sniffing cocaine, and even smoking opium. He knew that Archie would kill him if he didn't kill Archie first.

The next day Malcolm wandered down St. Nicholas Avenue in Harlem. He heard a horn. High, nervous, and scared, he thought it was a gun. He spun round and pulled out his gun. He couldn't believe his eyes—it was his friend Shorty. Sammy had heard that Malcolm was in real trouble. He had called Shorty in Boston and told him to come and get Malcolm out of town.

Within minutes, Malcolm had packed the few possessions he had into Shorty's car trunk, and they were headed back to Boston. It would be 10 years before Malcolm returned to Harlem. The home that he had built for himself in Harlem had now also collapsed.

5
A STOLEN WATCH

> ❝ *Looking back, I think I really was at least slightly out of my mind. I viewed narcotics as most people regard food. I wore my guns as today I wear my neckties...I think I deliberately invited death in many, sometimes insane ways.* ❞
>
> **MALCOLM X**

Malcolm sat on the edge of the bed and emptied all the bullets out of his gun. Then he carefully placed one bullet back in, spun the chamber around, and lifted the gun to his head. "Click" went the gun as Malcolm pulled the trigger.

Shorty, another friend called Rudy, and the two women in the room couldn't believe what they were seeing. All four of them just sat there with their mouths wide open. Shorty and Rudy got ready to jump Malcolm, and the women pleaded with him to stop. "Click," Malcolm pulled again, and "click" for the third time. He was playing a game called Russian roulette. Then he stopped.

"I'm doing this, showing you I'm not afraid to die," he told them. "Never cross a man not afraid to die ... now, let's get to work!"

"Work" was stealing. Back in Boston, Malcolm had organized a small group of thieves. It had taken him a while to recover from the nightmare he left behind in Harlem. He had moved in with Shorty and slept for days. When he was awake, he just sat in Shorty's home smoking reefers and staring into space. After two or three weeks, he had found someone who could supply him with cocaine, and this made him feel like talking again. Sophia and Malcolm had gotten together again, and her sister was now going out with Shorty.

Malcolm needed to make money. His cocaine habit cost him $20 a day. This was a fortune in 1945. He suggested burglary and Shorty jumped at the idea. Rudy also wanted to be a part of the burglaries. Even Sophia and her sister wanted to join in.

It was on their first night that Malcolm had frightened the group by playing Russian roulette with his gun. He knew that from then on they would do exactly what he told them to do. What the four of them never knew was that Malcolm had cheated. He made it look as if he had put that bullet into the gun. In actual fact, though, he had slipped the bullet into the palm of his hand. Playing Russian roulette was a foolish thing to do, even though there was no risk when he pulled the trigger.

The team worked well together. Now and then Rudy worked as a waiter in the houses of wealthy neighborhoods. He knew which houses would make good targets for them. But the two people who really made this little band of thieves successful were Sophia and her sister. They acted as "finders"—finding places for the men to steal from. No one suspected anything when the two women came around knocking at doors. They pretended to be saleswomen or college women taking a survey.

Once inside, they started out by saying how beautiful the house was. After that, the owner was usually so pleased that he or she took them all over the house. When they were back home they drew a map of the house for Malcolm, Shorty, and Rudy. The map showed which rooms they should enter and where the valuable things were kept. The three men returned at night with small flashlights. They slipped in through a window or door, gathered what they wanted, and then left—sometimes with the people asleep in their beds! For a few months, the burglaries went as smoothly as they could have hoped.

Then Malcolm broke the team's golden rule: Never keep anything you steal, and sell everything as fast as you can. It was a watch and it was so beautiful that he just had to have it. The owner of the watch had told the police that his watch had been stolen. He also told them that it needed to be repaired. It was a very expensive watch, he had explained, and it would be easy to recognize. The police had alerted all the jewelers in Boston to look out for this watch.

Of course Malcolm took the watch to be fixed. When he went to pick it up, the police were waiting. It didn't take them long to round up Sophia and her sister and drag Shorty off the bandstand where he was playing with his band that night. They never caught Rudy. Somehow he heard about what had happened and fled from Boston. The police found all sorts of evidence in the gang's apartment. It wasn't difficult to prove what they had been doing.

Malcolm stood quietly in the Middlesex County court that day in February 1946. He had been caught, and all his clever hustles and tricks were no use now. Handcuffed before the judge, Malcolm listened to what his sentence was:

"Not less than 5 years, and no more than 10...."

Ten years! Malcolm's lawyers could not believe their ears. People got 10 years for crimes that were much worse. For robbery, the sentence was usually about three years.

Although his lawyers were puzzled, Malcolm knew exactly

why his sentence was so harsh. He knew, before the judge had even spoken, that his real crime was that he had mixed with white women. He knew that white people saw this as a crime much worse than robbery. "Goddamn niggers ..." he heard someone whisper in the courtroom. Shorty received a similar sentence, and Sophia and her sister got one to five years.

Malcolm's life had been destroyed once again. He was not yet 21 years old. He hadn't even started to shave.

Malcolm was sent to Charlestown State Prison, a prison that could only be described as a pit. The cells there were so small that Malcolm could lie on his cot and touch both walls with his arms. There was no running water. There were no bathrooms, just buckets. And there were bars everywhere.

Malcolm was addicted to drugs, and now he was forced to do without them. He was always miserable and in a bad mood. First he started cursing God. Then he started swearing at all the prison guards. He refused to answer when his number was called. He threw his food on the floor. Because of his behavior, Malcolm was punished. He was placed in solitary confinement. This meant that he would be in an even smaller cell and would have no privileges at all.

Malcolm's nickname changed while he was in prison. Outside he had been known as Detroit Red. In prison, they began to call him Satan because he cursed God all the time. He began to get high on a spice he got from the prison kitchens. And then, when he got money from Ella, he bought more powerful drugs from the prison guards. He was getting used to his new life.

But Bimbi changed everything. He was also an African American, and a burglar who had been in several prisons before. Malcolm first met Bimbi in the machine shop, where they both worked stamping out license plates for cars. After work Bimbi just talked. Everyone sat around and listened. Bimbi could talk about anything—history, God, governments, even ideas. Malcolm was impressed by how softly Bimbi spoke. He was also envious of how Bimbi got so many people to listen to him. Malcolm got attention by swearing and cursing, but Bimbi got so much more respect from people by his soft words of wisdom. Malcolm stopped swearing.

"What fascinated me with him most of all was that he was the first man I had ever seen command total respect ... with his words," Malcolm told a friend many years later.

Bimbi noticed how Malcolm listened to him. He could tell that Malcolm understood things. Use your brain, he told Malcolm. Don't let it rot in here—it's the only thing you have that's yours to do with as you please. Malcolm wanted friendship more than advice. But he listened, and he acted. He began to learn English all over again, and he took college courses through the mail. He was determined to educate himself.

Malcolm had dropped out of school in the eighth grade and had forgotten almost everything he had ever learned. It wasn't easy to start all over again, and all by himself. Slowly but surely, the rules of grammar came back to him, and after about a year he was able to write a decent letter to Ella. Malcolm was also fascinated with languages. He became interested in the origin of words, or where words come from and what their original meaning was. He took a course in Latin, a language that is no longer spoken, but is the origin of most of the words in the English language.

Malcolm took no notice when he got a strange letter from his brother Philbert. Philbert told Malcolm that he had found the "natural religion for the black man" and it was called the Nation of Islam. Religion was the last thing Malcolm was interested in. He didn't care about God. If there was a God, why was he there in prison? In any case, Philbert was always joining some crazy new group; and Malcolm didn't want to be a part of it.

A few weeks later, Malcolm received another letter. This one was from Reginald. Malcolm respected Reginald more than he did any of his other brothers. In his letter, Reginald wrote: "Malcolm, don't eat any more pork, and don't smoke any more cigarettes. I'll show you how to get out of prison."

Malcolm couldn't understand what Reginald meant. Would not doing these things make him so ill that he would be released? It was a total mystery, but Malcolm didn't care. He would do anything to get out. Small news was big news in prison. When Malcolm gave up pork and cigarettes, no one could figure it out. Then Malcolm got lucky. In late 1948, Ella somehow managed to get him sent to a jail called the Norfolk Prison Colony. This jail was like an experiment. There were no bars, he had his own room, it was less crowded, there was more light, and there were even real bathrooms. Compared with the first two prisons, this was heaven.

Every evening there were discussions and debates. There was also a library that had been donated by a millionaire named Mr. Parkhurst. This man had taken an interest in the unusual programs at Norfolk and had given all of his books to help the prisoners learn. Most of these books were about history and religion. Malcolm started reading more and more. But he never forgot what Reginald had said to him. When Reginald wrote and told Malcolm that he was coming to visit in a few weeks, Malcolm couldn't wait to find out what his brother had meant.

 # THE MESSAGE OF ALLAH

> ❝ It was right there in prison that I made up my mind to devote the rest of my life to telling the white man about himself—or die. ❞
>
> **MALCOLM X, The Autobiography of Malcolm X**

❝**M**alcolm, if a man knew every imaginable thing that there is to know, who would he be?" Reginald asked when he finally came to visit.

Malcolm thought for a while and then said, "Well, he would have to be some kind of a god."

Reginald nodded. "There's a man who knows everything. God is a man," he said. "His real name is Allah."

Malcolm was quiet. This religious talk was a surprise—especially from Reginald, who had never been a religious person like Philbert. But Malcolm sat and listened.

Reginald spoke softly. He told his older brother that God has 360 degrees of knowledge, just as a circle has 360 degrees. So God has the "sum total of knowledge." Malcolm began to get confused, but still he listened.

Reginald told Malcolm that the devil has only 33 degrees of knowledge and that he uses this to rule other people. Then Reginald really surprised Malcolm.

"The devil is also a man," he said. Then he pointed to the white prisoners and prison guards in the room. "Them," he whispered. "The *white* man is the devil." Reginald told Malcolm that God had come to America, that he had made himself known to an African American called Elijah Poole. God had told Mr. Poole that the devil's time was up.

By the time Reginald had left, Malcolm's head was swimming with strange, new thoughts. He didn't know what to think. As far as Malcolm was concerned, how could he be in this mess if there was a God? And also, what about getting him out of prison? Malcolm had forgotten to ask his brother Reginald about all that.

Then Malcolm began to think seriously about what Reginald had said. He thought about all the white people in his life. He thought about the people who had burned down his family's house and murdered his father. He thought about the welfare department, which had broken up his family and sent his mother to the hospital. He thought of the Swerlins and school, and how they had never accepted him as a person. He thought of Mr. Ostrowski, his English teacher, of the white criminals in Harlem, and finally he thought of the people who had thrown him into jail. Maybe Reginald was right! It seemed to him that all the pain and hurt he had ever suffered had been caused by white people.

Malcolm had so many more questions to ask Reginald. He couldn't wait for his brother to come back. When Reginald did return, he talked for two hours, softly telling his big brother what he saw as the truth:

"You don't even know who you are. You don't even know, the white devil has hidden it from you, that you are a race of people of ancient civilizations and riches in gold and kings. You don't even know your true family name, you wouldn't recognize your true language if you heard it. You have been cut off by the devil white man from all knowledge of your own kind. You have been a victim of the evil of the devil white man ever since he murdered and raped and stole you from your native land in the seeds of your forefathers...."

Malcolm had never heard anyone talk like this before. He sat quietly, listening to Reginald until it was time for him to leave.

While he was in prison, Malcolm got lots of letters and visits from his family—especially from Reginald. Through these visits, Malcolm began to learn about a religion called Islam and the church that supported a version of it in America: the Nation of Islam. This is the story he learned:

On July 4, 1930, God appeared in the shape of a man called Wallace D. Fard. Fard sold expensive silks from all over the world in the run-down black parts of Detroit. He became well known because he told people beautiful stories about their ancient African homelands. He preached against the white race and also against the Christian religion. At first people thought he was a preacher or a minister. Then he performed certain miracles, and the people who listened to and believed in him grew. Mr. Fard organized the very first temple for this new religion. He also built schools. In Detroit, Mr. Fard had chosen Elijah Poole as his "messenger." Mr. Poole was instructed by Mr. Fard to build the religion and spread its message. But in 1934, Mr. Fard disappeared. The small, delicate Elijah Poole, the son of a poor farmer from Georgia, took over.

Elijah Poole told everyone that Mr. Fard had been God. He said that God (as Mr. Fard) had come to the United States to make all African Americans aware of their natural religion and to make them rise up against their devil slave masters—the white people. Their natural religion was not Christianity. It was

Elijah Muhammad, leader of the Nation of Islam and at one time Malcolm X's spiritual leader.

an old religion from the East called Islam. God was called Allah. If you believed in Islam and Allah, you were known as a Muslim.

Elijah Poole changed his name to Elijah Muhammad and called himself the Messenger. He taught that history had been "whitened," that the peoples of Africa had been fed the white man's version of who they are for thousands of years. He taught that in the beginning, long before Adam and Eve, the moon broke away from the earth. Then the first race of humans was created. They were black, he said. You can't make black from white, he said, but you can get white from black. This proved that black people *must* have been first.

The Messenger taught that white people were created through an experiment by an angry scientist who had been sent away to an island for causing trouble. He had bred a race of "white devils" to upset the peace of the world and get revenge.

The white devils destroyed the great civilizations of anyone who wasn't white. This destruction was written down in many history books.

Elijah Muhammad taught about how wealthy and advanced these black nations had been. He pointed to the evidence that was being dug up in Africa, and to the great civilizations of Ethiopia and Egypt. He taught that the devil white man had kidnapped millions of black men, women, and children and brought them to America. It was written, he preached, that after 6,000 years of white rule, a messenger would arrive to wake up this "Lost-Found Nation" of black people in America. They would then destroy the white race of devils. Mr. Muhammad claimed that those 6,000 years were now up.

Alone in prison, Malcolm didn't know what to believe. He knew that the Bible had stories in it that sounded just as strange as what Mr. Muhammad was teaching. Why should he believe any of these stories? He began to wonder what it all meant. What he heard seemed to offer some real answers to his questions for the very first time. It gave his life meaning and hope. For the first time, he was beginning to understand why he was in jail, and why he had done the things he had done. He began to believe that it wasn't because he was a bad person. It was because the white devils had given him no choice.

Malcolm threw himself into these new ideas. He began to write to Elijah Muhammad and was amazed when Mr. Muhammad wrote back answering his questions and telling him more about the religious explanations of what had really happened in history. He also began to find some things out for himself. He went to the library to see what was written in the history books. But he found that he couldn't understand what many of the words meant. Then he began to copy a page out of the dictionary every day. Every day he tried to copy another page of the dictionary into his notebook. When the lights went out at ten o'clock, he would read by the dim light of a lamp in the hall. In fact, he strained his eyes so much over the next few years that he had to wear glasses for the rest of his life.

"Ten guards and the warden couldn't have torn me out of those books," Malcolm remembered. He read about the great black civilizations in Africa. He read about the horror of slavery. He saw pictures of slave ships in which slaves were chained and sold as if they were animals.

The change that came over Malcolm while he was in prison could not have been more surprising. From a cursing street hustler, he had turned into an intelligent and thoughtful man who seemed to have mastered the power of words. He was also following the strict rules of Elijah Muhammad's religion, which did not allow swearing, smoking, drinking, or eating pork. Malcolm later admitted that he thought he got more out of prison than anyone ever had. In prison, unlike a school or col-

Malcolm X (second from right) with fellow Muslims during his early days with the Nation of Islam.

lege, he had all of his time to himself. He could learn and focus his attention without being distracted.

By 1952, the prison authorities decided that Malcolm could leave. He had been in prison for seven years. Malcolm walked out of those prison gates with a new suit and $10 in his pocket. He was going to forget his old street-hustling ways—he had chosen a different life now. He would have to start over again. This time he would build a new house with a stronger foundation.

SPREADING THE WORD

❝God has given Mr. Muhammad some sharp truth, it is like a two-edged sword. It cuts into you. It causes you great pain, but if you can take the truth, it will cure you and save you from what otherwise would be certain death.❞

MALCOLM X, *The Autobiography of Malcolm X*

Malcolm spent hours in a steam bath that first day of freedom. Sitting there, sweating all those years of prison dirt out of his body, he felt that he was also steaming away some of his painful prison memories. He then went to Detroit to live with his brother Wilfred's family. Wilfred had promised Malcolm a job and a place in which to live. He had also promised to introduce his brother to the Nation of Islam.

Malcolm began to work in a furniture store where Wilfred was the manager. The store was in a black neighborhood, but it was owned by whites. The furniture wasn't of very good

Malcolm X became active in the Nation of Islam soon after his release from prison.

quality, but the store allowed people to buy things on credit and pay for them over a long period of time. Some people never realized how expensive this really was. By the time they had finished paying for something on this credit, they ended up paying twice what the furniture actually cost.

Malcolm saw how his brothers and sisters were being cheated by the store owners. "Now I watched brothers entwining themselves in [falling into] the economic clutches of the white man who went home every night with another bag of the money drained out of the ghetto." It made him angry. If only the African Americans in this part of town could own all the stores, he thought to himself. That way the money would go back into the community, not into the pockets of people who lived elsewhere and had no interest in helping the community.

But Malcolm was happy to be working. It was good just to be out of prison. Wilfred's family taught Malcolm all about Muslim family life. It was a polite, respectful household. There were routines about getting up and washing. Each person washed thoroughly, as is the Muslim tradition. Everyone greeted each other at the beginning of the day with "*As-salaam-alaikum,*" which means "peace be with you" in the Arabic language (Islam came from Arabia). Prayer was an important part of the day. Wilfred spread a prayer rug and the whole family knelt down, facing the East. They would softly praise Allah together and then go off to work. For Malcolm, this time was "a healing change from the prison cage."

Malcolm was taken to the Detroit Temple Number One. In the Nation of Islam, all the temples, or churches, have a number. Since this was where the religion began in the United States under Wallace D. Fard, this church was number one. It was only a small storefront church, but it was all the people needed. Malcolm met other Muslims. He was impressed with how polite and well dressed everyone was. He noticed how Muslims greeted one another with respect and affection. "I had never dreamed of anything like that [feeling] among black people who had learned to be proud they were black, who had learned to love other black people instead of being jealous and suspicious," Malcolm said.

Malcolm was also very interested in the minister who spread the word of Allah at the Detroit Temple Number One. Minister Lemuel Hassan stood before a blackboard teaching about Islam and the fall of the black man. Malcolm had done a lot of studying about the religion on his own. Now he wanted to hear these ideas preached!

Malcolm believed so strongly that what he was hearing was the truth. Why, then, were there so many empty seats in the temple? He complained to his brother that there should be no empty seats when there were so many brothers and sisters drinking, cursing, fighting, dancing, and using drugs in the streets outside. But at Temple Number One, Minister Lemuel felt that Allah Himself would bring in more Muslims. He felt that the temple should be there for them, and that in the meantime they should wait for any new members to walk through the doors.

Now Malcolm wasn't the kind of man who liked to wait for anything. He also felt that he knew the streets better than anyone else there. He knew that people wouldn't just turn up.

On the Sunday before Labor Day in 1952, 10 cars set out from Detroit Temple Number One. They were going to Chicago, to Temple Number Two, to hear the Messenger speak.

Malcolm could hardly sit still. After all these years of learning about this amazing man, he was actually going to see him and hear him talk. He hadn't felt so excited since he was a small boy. When they arrived, they all crowded into the temple and waited for the Messenger.

Elijah Muhammad appeared from the back of the temple and walked up to the front. There was silence. Most Muslims there had seen the Messenger before, but not Malcolm. Malcolm noticed how small and sensitive the Messenger seemed to be. Members of the Fruit of Islam were all around him. Compared with them, he seemed so tiny. They all wore dark suits, white shirts, and bow ties. The Messenger was wearing a small hat on his head that looked a bit like a bowl that had been turned upside down. The hat, called a fez, was beautiful. It was covered with gold stitching.

Not only was this the first time Malcolm saw Mr. Muhammad, it was also the first time he saw the Fruit of Islam. These were members of the Nation of Islam who were trained to help organize meetings, keep order, and protect the Messenger and all the other people who belonged to the Nation of Islam.

Malcolm listened very carefully to Elijah Muhammad as he spoke. Mr. Muhammad talked softly and slowly. But every word seemed so clear, so true! He told of how he had been preaching over the years, and of the time he had spent in prison for refusing to fight in the white man's war. He also talked about the "blue-eyed devil white man" who had managed to brainwash the black people of America until they were "mentally, morally and spiritually dead." He stopped to take a short rest. Malcolm couldn't believe that so much force and power could come from such a small, gentle-looking man. Then Mr. Muhammad called Malcolm's name.

Malcolm was scared. How did the Messenger of Allah even know that he was there? Malcolm had no time to think. In a second, he was on his feet in front of 200 Muslims.

The Messenger told everyone about Malcolm and how strong he had been in prison. "Every day, and for years, Brother Malcolm has written a letter from prison to me. And I have written to him as often as I could," he announced. Then he challenged Malcolm to prove to everyone that he had really discovered Allah. Would he give in to the devil now that he was out of prison and go back to his old ways of drinking and crime? he asked. The Messenger didn't think so. "I believe that he is going to remain faithful," he said.

That night Mr. Muhammad invited Malcolm and other members from the Detroit temple to share dinner with him at his house. Malcolm was nervous. During dinner he hardly said a word. Then he asked the Messenger how many people should be at the Detroit temple.

"Thousands," came the reply. Malcolm knew it! You can't just expect them to come, you have to go and get them. He made up his mind to bring more people into the Nation of Islam.

Back in Detroit, Malcolm spent every spare minute he had going fishing—fishing for new members on the streets of Detroit, that is. Many people didn't want to listen. Malcolm was upset when he found out how difficult it was to make people listen to the teachings of Mr. Muhammad. Slowly but surely, though, his hard work was rewarded. Soon, Malcolm and the other Muslims who had been "fishing" managed to triple the membership of their small temple.

Malcolm was formally accepted into the Nation of Islam and received his "X." This *X* replaced Little, the name his white slave masters had given his ancestors. The *X* stood for his true African family name that he could never know—never know, that is, until Allah returned it to him, taught the Messenger.

Malcolm X's relationship with the Messenger grew as well. Mr. Muhammad knew that he had an eager and smart young man who could help spread the word of Allah. And Malcolm X greatly admired Mr. Muhammad.

It wasn't long before Malcolm X was asked by Minister Hassan to speak to members of the Detroit temple. He wasn't sure if he could do it. He had debated before, but he had never preached the word of Allah. He agreed, though, and he spoke about Christianity and slavery:

"My brothers and sisters, our white slavemaster's Christian religion has taught us black people here in the wilderness of North America that we will sprout wings when we die and fly up into the sky where God will have for us a special place called heaven. This is [the] white man's Christian religion used to *brainwash* us black people! We have *accepted* it! We have *embraced* it! We have *believed* it! We have *practiced* it! And while we are doing all of that, for himself, this blue-eyed devil has twisted his Christianity, to keep his *foot* on our backs ... to keep our eyes fixed on the pie in the sky and heaven in the hereafter ... while *he* enjoys *his* heaven right *here* ... on *this earth* ... in *this* life."

Malcolm X spoke well, and everyone noticed. His sharp and intelligent tongue brought the message of Mr. Muhammad to life. By the summer of 1953, he was made the assistant minister to the Detroit temple. Every day he was out on the streets trying to interest more people in the Nation of Islam. He couldn't wait for Minister Lemuel to let him speak again. And the more he spoke, the more he realized the truth that he was discovering for himself and sharing with others. "I would become so choked up that sometimes I would walk in the streets until late into the night," he said. "Sometimes I would speak to no one for hours, thinking to myself about what the white man had done to our poor people here in America."

Malcolm had changed jobs a few times since he had been living in Detroit. He was now working for the Ford Motor Company, helping to put their cars together. But he left that job to devote all of his time to the Messenger and to become a full-time minister. It was an important decision. Malcolm began spending all of his time in Chicago with Mr. Muhammad. He learned many things about the religion of Islam. He learned how to pray. He learned how the Nation of Islam was organized and run. He studied the Koran, the holy book of the Islamic religion. In some ways, Elijah Muhammad became the father who had been taken from Malcolm back in 1931.

Mr. Muhammad first sent Malcolm to Boston to see if he could get enough people interested to start a temple there. Malcolm worked hard on the streets to get people to come to meetings that he had arranged in someone's home or in a hall. He always began by talking about the horrors of slavery. He knew that would get people interested. Then he eased out of slavery and into religion. He talked about how the white devil's crimes had caught up with him, and how it was time for African

Americans to stand up and take back what was rightfully theirs. The Muslim message was clear. They believed there should be full rights and full equality for everybody. "God has given Mr. Muhammad some sharp truth," he would say. "It is like a two-edged sword. It cuts into you. It causes you great pain, but if you can take the truth, it will cure you and save you from what otherwise would be certain death." Now and then Malcolm would see Ella in the group of people that had gathered to listen, but she never joined the temple. He also dropped in on Shorty, who was also out of prison. Shorty didn't want to hear anything about religion, but he was happy to see Malcolm again.

After three months in Boston, Malcolm had opened the eyes of enough people to begin a small temple. He was so proud when he told Mr. Muhammad the good news!

Mr. Muhammad knew right from the start how useful Malcolm would be in spreading the message of Allah. Malcolm was young, attractive, and able to speak very clearly. He seemed to have a very special kind of energy. People were drawn to him. As soon as the Boston temple was set up, Malcolm was moved to Philadelphia to start a temple there. Within three months, Malcolm had set up another temple.

Then Mr. Muhammad asked Malcolm to take up the biggest challenge of all. He asked him to go right into the heart of the African-American community in the United States. This was a place where more African Americans lived than anywhere else in the United States—more than 1 million at that time. This was a place that the Nation of Islam had to conquer if it was going to really expand the way the Messenger and Malcolm wanted it to. Mr. Muhammad asked Malcolm X to go to Harlem in New York City.

HARLEM AND MONTGOMERY

> *❝ There comes a time when people get tired. We are here this evening to say to those who have mistreated us so long that we are tired—tired of being segregated and humiliated; tired of being kicked about by the brutal feet of oppression... ❞*

MARTIN LUTHER KING, JR.

Old memories flooded Malcolm X's mind as he wandered down the familiar streets of Harlem. It was June 1954. He remembered the guns, the drugs, the hustlers—the fear. How his life had changed! What would they think of him now?

Malcolm looked at Harlem through different eyes. Instead of an eager street hustler, he was now an important minister for a growing religion. He used to wear zoot suits and big hats. Now he wore a simple dark suit with a white shirt and a necktie. He also wore glasses. And his hair was curly again—no conking for Malcolm ever again. In the old days, Malcolm was easily impressed by the glamour of the ghetto. Now he was a serious, thoughtful man—a man with a mission. He was a man who had returned to Harlem to change the ways of its people rather than to take advantage of them.

He visited a couple of his old hangouts and found some friends from his hustling days. His friends could hardly believe what they saw. There stood Malcolm! He found West Indian Archie, and they made up. Maybe both of them had been wrong about those numbers. Anyway, it hardly mattered now.

Delivering Harlem to Allah wasn't as easy as Malcolm thought it would be. The New York Temple Number Seven was only a little storefront. Most of the people in Harlem had never heard of the Nation of Islam. They didn't even know what the word *Muslim* meant.

Malcolm X realized that Harlem was overflowing with many other groups that were trying to attract members. There were nationalist groups, like the followers of Marcus Garvey, who were also telling black people how they had been mistreated. There was Christianity, too—hundreds of different churches trying to increase their flocks. Malcolm X had to think of some way of competing with all these other religions in Harlem.

Malcolm's plans were simple. First he had information printed up. Then he handed it out on street corners with a group of other Muslims from the temple. "Hear how the white man kidnapped and robbed and raped our black race," they shouted. Then they went "fishing" among the crowds of people who had gathered to listen to other speakers in Harlem! Slowly, new faces began to turn up at the temple. The greatest success they had was among the Christian churches. As soon as the people came out of those churches, Malcolm and his friends pounced. "You haven't heard anything until you have heard the teachings of the Honorable Elijah Muhammad," the Muslims shouted. Malcolm had arranged the temple's meetings for two o'clock every Sunday so that they wouldn't interfere with the morning Christian services.

Knowing that there were many Christians who had come to listen to him preach, Malcolm spoke about things they would easily understand. He talked of how the Christian religion had been used to keep African Americans down. He told them to look around. He invited them to wander through Manhattan. Christianity, Malcolm explained, tried to tell blacks not to mind if they weren't equal. It told them to stop worrying about their suffering because they would be rewarded in heaven. But in the meantime, Malcolm said, look who was enjoying all the wealth and privileges here on earth—whites!

Malcolm often used simple stories to make it easier for people to understand what he was trying to say. "I had learned early one important thing, and that was to always teach in terms that the people could understand," he said. After each speech, he asked all those who believed what he had said to stand up. Everyone did. But when he asked those people who wanted to follow Elijah Muhammad to stand, only one or two did, and sometimes none at all.

Malcolm knew it was the Muslim rules that kept people away. There was no smoking, drinking, dancing, or drugs. No dating. No lying or stealing. No gambling, no sports, no movies, and no having sex with anyone except the person to whom you were married. This was why Temple Number Seven grew so slowly. Malcolm became impatient. He knew the good that he could bring. He began traveling from one part of the country to another. He preached at established temples and helped start new ones—even in the South. Malcolm did so much traveling that the Nation of Islam bought him a car. Within five months, he had traveled more than 30,000 miles.

By 1956, the Nation of Islam had grown considerably—especially in the big cities like Detroit, Chicago, and New York. As more people joined, the group became more powerful and wealthy. It was gaining strength and popularity.

Another African-American movement was also becoming widely known by 1956. It also spoke of the injustices done to blacks. It also talked of lack of equality, but it was very different from the Nation of Islam. Instead of growing in the North like the Nation of Islam, this movement was growing mostly in the South. Instead of talking about an independent, separate nation for blacks, it talked about integration and acceptance—sharing schools and hospitals equally with whites. And instead of being based on Islam and the destruction of the whites, it was based on Christianity and loving the enemy. Even though these two movements were struggling for the same thing—the freedom and equality of blacks—its members disagreed on the best way of achieving their goals.

Movements among African Americans had been organized ever since the Africans had been kidnapped and brought to America as slaves. One important organization, the National Association for the Advancement of Colored People (NAACP), had been fighting for African-American rights since the beginning of the century. Many of its leaders were lawyers. They believed that they could make the courts see how unfair things were in the United States. By changing the laws, they thought they could make things better for African Americans.

The NAACP lawyers won one of their most important cases in 1954. They took this case to the most powerful court in the country, the United States Supreme Court. The case was called *Brown* v. *Board of Education*. The Supreme Court ruled that having separate schools for whites and blacks was unfair. It was unfair because the white schools were better than the black schools. It was unfair because it caused black children to think they were not as good as white children. The Court ruled that segregation in any school was against the U.S. Constitution and was therefore illegal.

The Supreme Court recognized that segregation *anywhere* was wrong. It would be just a matter of time and money before the NAACP could bring other cases of segregation to the Court and win. This meant that the old law of the land, which allowed segregation, would be changed. But the Supreme Court left it up to each state to enforce the new laws. Some of the states didn't want to change their ways, and they ignored the Supreme Court ruling. They weren't going to do anything until they were forced to.

The following year, 1955, two very important things happened. The first was the murder of Emmett Till. Emmett Till was a 14-year-old boy from Chicago. He had been sent to Mississippi for the summer to stay with his cousin. He didn't realize how different the South was from the North. As a dare among his friends, he had approached a white woman in a grocery store and said "Bye, baby" to her. According to reports, later that day the woman's husband and two friends turned up where Emmett was staying and forced him into getting in their car. Emmett's body was found three days later. There was barbed wire around his neck; one eye was gouged out, his forehead was bashed in, and there was a bullet in his skull.

Emmett's mother was sick with grief. Like many people in the United States, she knew, things like this had been going on in the South for years. Thousands of African Americans had disappeared. In pain and anger, Mrs. Till was determined to show the world what was happening there. When Emmett's body arrived back in Chicago, she put it on public display. Within a few days, photographs of this poor boy's broken body were shown in a national magazine. Many people in the United States were angry at what they saw and heard. But the men who had kidnapped Emmett stayed free. They were never found guilty of his murder by the white judge and the white jury.

The second major event of that year came at the end of 1955. On December 1, Rosa Parks, a seamstress and NAACP member who lived in Montgomery, Alabama, boarded a city bus. Tired, she sat down in the middle of the bus, in the first seat she could find. The law in Montgomery said it was legal for blacks to sit there only until whites came on the bus and couldn't find

One of the many buses that traveled with no passengers during the Montgomery bus boycott.

seats in the front. Then blacks were supposed to stand and give up their seats.

When a white man got on the bus and there were no more seats for whites, the driver ordered Rosa Parks to get up. She refused. She knew the white man was no better than she was. The driver had her arrested.

Rosa Parks was taken to the police station, and word spread among the African-American leaders of Montgomery that another black person had been arrested. That night, E. D. Nixon, who had once been president of the local NAACP, asked Rosa Parks if they could take her case to the courts. Rosa Parks agreed.

Other African-American leaders in Montgomery decided to arrange a bus boycott. A boycott meant that none of the blacks would ride the buses. Since so many African Americans used the buses, they could destroy the bus company by not using it and giving it money. The first day of the boycott was a great success. Should they continue? The most important people in the African-American community called a meeting. They appointed a new, young minister to lead the boycott. Not many people had heard of him before. His name was Dr. Martin Luther King, Jr.

Dr. King was a natural leader and a wonderful speaker who was becoming an important figure in black people's struggle for equality, or civil rights. He was only 26, four years younger than Malcolm X. That night everyone agreed that they would go on with the boycott. The civil rights movement was gathering strength.

On December 20, 1956, more than a year after the boycott began, the Supreme Court ruling arrived in Montgomery: Bus segregation was illegal! The next day African Americans began to ride the buses again. From now on, everyone on the buses would be treated equally according to the law.

The Montgomery bus boycott wasn't just about letting people sit where they wanted to sit. It was the first time in the 1950s that the African-American community had organized itself on such a huge scale. The people of the community saw what they could achieve if they worked together. What's more, they did it without using violence.

When the boycott ended, Martin Luther King, Jr., and other Christian ministers set up an organization to give shape to their struggle. It was called the Southern Christian Leadership Conference (SCLC). Dr. King was elected president.

Back in Harlem, Malcolm was upset that so few people had heard of his movement. Everyone seemed to be listening to the radio and reading the papers about the bus boycott in Montgomery. But that was about to change.

A COUNTRY AWAKENS

❝ *And then, in that dim light, Malcolm stood up and waved his hand, and all those people just disappeared.* **Disappeared. One of the police people said to me, 'Did you see what I just saw?' I said, 'Yeah.' He said, 'This is too much power for one man to have.' He meant one black man. I'll never forget that.** ❞

JAMES HICKS, editor of *Amsterdam News*

❝**H**ey! Stop that!" shouted Brother Hinton, one of the temple brothers. It was a cold April evening in 1957, and Hinton was on his way home. He had turned the corner, and there was a policeman hitting and beating a man. Hinton didn't know what had happened. But he did know that the policeman had no right to hit the man so hard when he wasn't fighting back.

"Go away!" shouted the policeman. Hinton refused. The policeman turned and went for Hinton. He raised his club: "Thwack!" He hit Hinton in the head with all his might, splitting his scalp with the club. Hinton crumpled to the ground. The police put him into a van and took him to the station.

Incidents like this weren't unusual in Harlem. The police had been known to use more violence than they had to and get away with it. But this time, another member of the temple had seen the whole thing happen, and he called Malcolm. Malcolm made other calls, and within half an hour 50 of the temple's Fruit of Islam were standing outside the police station. It was an impressive sight—50 men in suits and ties standing at attention as though they were in the army. Most people in Harlem couldn't believe what they were seeing!

Word spread fast. More and more people turned up to see what would happen. They wanted "some action." By the time Malcolm was able to talk to the police, more than 2,000 people had gathered outside the station. When Malcolm saw Hinton, he got very upset. Hinton's face was covered with blood. The police agreed to send him to Harlem Hospital immediately. "Now will you get rid of that crowd?" they asked. The police were scared. Malcolm walked outside and with one wave, the crowd seemed to disappear. The police stood there in amazement.

The story spread through Harlem like wildfire. Nobody had a private army like this young minister from the Nation of Islam. Everyone in Harlem wanted to know who these Muslims were. More and more people began turning up at the temple.

For the past three years, Malcolm had devoted all of his time and energy to Mr. Muhammad and the Nation of Islam. In fact, he had hardly had any time to himself. But something in his personal life began to take up more and more of his time. Malcolm X had met Sister Betty X.

Sister Betty taught nursing to the other Muslim sisters on Thursday nights at the temple. She also worked at one of the big

Malcolm X with two of his children and his wife, Betty Shabazz, a sister in the Nation of Islam.

New York hospitals. Soon Malcolm couldn't stop thinking about her. He found himself dropping in on her classes more and more.

Betty couldn't stop thinking about Malcolm either. But she knew that her upper-class family from Detroit wouldn't approve. "What on earth are my parents going to say when I bring this dude home?" she kept wondering.

On his way to see his brother in Detroit, Malcolm decided that he had had enough. He pulled into a gas station, ran over to the phone, and fumbled in his pocket for enough change to make a call. "Look, do you want to get married?" he blurted out to Betty.

Malcolm and Betty were married on January 14, 1958, in Lansing, Michigan, his hometown. Betty was right about her family. They wouldn't even talk to her after the marriage. When they got back to New York, they moved in with another Muslim brother in Queens. Their first child was born in November. They named her Attallah. Shortly after Attallah's birth, they moved to a seven-room house in East Elmhurst—an African-American section of New York City in Queens.

Although the case of Brother Hinton had made people in Harlem aware of the Muslims, most of the whites in America had never heard of them. As far as they were concerned, the civil rights movement was taking place only in the South. There battles were being fought every day as blacks struggled for the right to enjoy the same privileges given to whites.

A dramatic example of one such battle took place in 1957 at the Central High School in Little Rock, Arkansas. Three years after the Supreme Court ruling in *Brown* v. *Board of Education*, the school board decided that it was time to begin integrating the schools in Little Rock. At that time there were separate schools for black children and separate, better schools for white children. Integrating the schools would allow both black and white children to attend the same schools and get the same kind of education.

Students being escorted to Central High School in Little Rock, Arkansas, on September 25, 1957.

The governor of Arkansas, Orville Faubus, didn't want black students in the white schools, so he sent in the state police with rifles and guns to keep them out. The children thought the police were there to protect them. But when they tried to get past, the state police blocked their way. There was a mob of white people who were shouting and screaming at them. Elizabeth Eckford was one of the children who were trying to get into the school. She was alone, in the middle of the angry crowd. "I tried to see a friendly face somewhere in the mob...." she remembered. "I looked into the face of an old woman, and it seemed a kind face, but when I looked at her again, she spat on me."

Finally, President Dwight Eisenhower had to send in the National Guard. The state was refusing to do what the Supreme Court had decreed was the law of the land. The whole world watched as nine children were taken to school every morning by the army with machine guns and rifles.

The message was loud and clear: Most whites in the South didn't want to integrate the schools and other public places. It became obvious that the battle for equal rights wouldn't be won overnight. Jim Crow and the laws of segregation would have to be fought and defeated one by one.

For all the whites in the country who thought that the civil rights movement was going on only in the South, two things happened in the North to change their thinking. First a program appeared on TV, then a book was published.

The TV program was called "The Hate That Hate Produced." It was about the Nation of Islam. Mr. Muhammad, Malcolm X, and the Muslims had cooperated in the project. They had allowed cameras into their meetings and rallies, and they gave interviews. Not much later, a book was published called *The Black Muslims in America*, written by Eric Lincoln.

Many people in America were shocked. Here was a group of people who said that white people were the devil. This group believed that one day African Americans would rise up and destroy the white civilization. Most important, they saw that the Nation of Islam wasn't just a strange little group. It was a popular, well-organized movement among thousands of African Americans. This, many white people suddenly realized, was much more of a threat than the civil rights movement in the South.

That year, 1959, almost every publication in the United States wanted to do a story on the Muslims. Magazines and newspapers wrote articles about the Nation of Islam. Radio and TV talk-show hosts wanted them on their programs. The person whom they wanted to interview more than anyone else was Malcolm X. He even started getting invitations to talk at famous universities, such as Harvard, Rutgers, and Brown. Malcolm could hardly believe it! He had only a homemade education, yet he was addressing some of the country's brightest minds.

Malcolm X holds Muhammad Speaks, *the Nation of Islam's paper, as he rallies support for freedom.*

Malcolm was determined to show that the Muslims weren't just a strange and small following. He showed how the teachings of the Islamic religion were no more incredible than those of the Christian religion. He wanted to tell people that the followers of the Nation of Islam had a good reason for preaching their message of hate. Their anger was a long-overdue reaction to the injustices that the whites had done to the blacks of America for so many years. "For the white man to ask the black man if he hates him is just like the raper asking the *raped*, or the wolf asking the *sheep*, 'Do you hate me?' The white man is in no moral position to accuse anyone else of hate!" exclaimed Malcolm.

In his interviews, the radio and newspaper people tried to trap Malcolm, and make him look like a black racist. This way they could say that he was no better than the white racists in the South who believed they were better than blacks.

"But Malcolm, why do you preach hate?" people from the newspapers asked.

"How can anybody ask us do we hate the white man who kidnapped us four hundred years ago, brought us here and stripped us of our history, stripped us of our culture, stripped us of our language, stripped us of everything you could have used today to prove that you're a part of the human family, bring you down to the level of an animal, sell you from plantation to plantation like a sack of wheat, sell you like a sack of potatoes, sell you like a horse and a plow, and then hung you up from one end of the country to the other, and then you ask me do I hate him? Why, your question is worthless!"

The radio and newspaper people were constantly comparing the Muslims to the "other" movement in the South. Malcolm jumped at the opportunity to answer them.

"What you don't realize, is that black people today don't think it is any victory to live next to you or enter your society. This is what you have to learn—that the black man has finally reached the point where he doesn't see what you have to offer. Today you haven't *got* anything to offer. Your own time has run out, your own ship is sinking, the seas are stormy, and now that your boat is rocking and on its way down, you're offering the black man a chance to integrate into your doomed society. And those Uncle Tom, brainwashed, white-minded Negroes who *love* you may do it, but the masses of black people want a society of their own in a land of their own."

Malcolm and the Muslims believed that to integrate would destroy the black race. They didn't want integration. They wanted total *separation*.

African Americans all over the country heard Malcolm. At last, many of them thought, here was someone who was clearly expressing their anger. The poor areas in the northern cities especially agreed with Malcolm's message. They couldn't escape their poverty because whites wouldn't give them a fair chance. Now here was someone who was saying that you didn't have to ask whites for anything anymore or even have anything to do with them.

Malcolm had become the spokesperson, or main speaker, for the Muslims and Elijah Muhammad. By now the Muslims had their own newspaper, *Muhammad Speaks*, which Malcolm had started. Their rallies were getting bigger and bigger. They hired the biggest arenas they could find and brought in Muslims from all over the country by bus. Ten thousand people or more went to meetings all over the country. They went to listen to Mr. Muhammad, who flew in from Chicago. "America had never seen such fantastic all-black meetings!" Malcolm said later. For him it was proof of the "power of Allah."

As the Nation of Islam grew, so did its wealth. By 1961, plans to build a $20 million Islamic Center in Chicago were announced. Two universities had been set up by the Nation of Islam. These universities carried children from kindergarten through junior-high school in Detroit and through high school in Chicago. Small Muslim-owned businesses succeeded and grew just as Mr. Muhammad had hoped they would.

But Mr. Muhammad's health took a turn for the worse. He was a frail man who had asthma, a condition that made it difficult for people to breathe. He often started coughing in the middle of a conversation and couldn't stop. He began to cancel his appearances.

Doctors recommended a dry climate for Mr. Muhammad, and the Nation of Islam bought a big house for him in Phoenix, Arizona. The Nation of Islam was more powerful now than it had ever been, and there's no doubt that the voice and energy of Malcolm X was responsible for much of that. But the good relations between Malcolm and the Nation of Islam would soon turn sour.

TRAPPED

> ❝ Malcolm's rage spluttered out into a depression that some of us took to be mourning; what we didn't know then was that he was grieving not only a lost brother but his own helplessness. ❞

PETER GOLDMAN, on Malcolm's reaction to the police shooting of a Muslim in Los Angeles: *The Life and Death of Malcolm X.*

The Muslims in the North waited for Allah to give them a sign. Meanwhile, the history of the civil rights movement was being shaped in the South.

African Americans continued to protest peacefully in the South by organizing sit-ins. The first sit-in took place in Greensboro, North Carolina, in early 1960. Many more soon followed as this way of rebelling against segregation popped up all over the South. In these sit-ins, a group of people, usually students, would sit in stores or lunch counters that were for whites only. Often angry whites came and threatened them with violence. They poured ketchup and hot coffee over the students' heads, for example. But the students didn't fight back—and they wouldn't move. Day in and day out, they came back until either the stores closed down altogether or began to serve people no matter what color their skin was.

To organize these sit-ins, the students had started their own group called the Student Nonviolent Coordinating Committee (SNCC). A courageous woman named Ella Baker had helped them. The large organizations, such as the NAACP, the SCLC, and the Congress of Racial Equality (CORE), had only a few people in control of making all the decisions. Often these people were lawyers or ministers. The SNCC was different. It was made up of all sorts of people. Most of them were young, many of them were students, and all of them had a say in how their group would make decisions.

Sit-ins weren't the only methods used to force local authorities to integrate, or desegregate, public places. The Freedom Rides were organized by CORE. On May 4, 1961, two buses set off from Washington, D.C., on a journey that would take them through the segregated South. Each bus was filled with both black and white people who were sitting wherever they wanted to sit. Such a mixed, or integrated, bus was now legal in the South as well as the North. In states like Mississippi and Alabama, however, public transportation was still segregated.

The Freedom Riders rode through the South trying to force the various states to accept the Supreme Court ruling against segregation in public transportation. The Freedom Rides sparked a violent reaction from racist southerners. Someone threw a fire bomb at one bus. Another bus was attacked by an angry mob in Birmingham, Alabama. There was another attack in Montgomery, where the police had secretly agreed to stay away for 15 minutes. During that time, both blacks and whites who were on the ride were beaten with lead pipes and baseball bats. Once again, the people of the United States had to witness shocking scenes of violence and brutality. They saw just how badly African Americans wanted their freedom—and how determined some white Americans were that they shouldn't have it. In the end, though, the Freedom Rides forced the bus companies to allow anyone to sit wherever he or she wanted to sit.

In Albany, Georgia, the movement tried to go a little further. There the marchers demonstrated in the city. They wanted to force the city government to change its rules about many different types of segregation, but they didn't succeed. They achieved nothing, and there were serious arguments among the different civil rights groups. Even Dr. King didn't seem to know what to do. "They didn't get anything but their heads whipped," Malcolm X mocked from New York.

But some people disagreed. They really believed that there was a revolution going on in the South. Malcolm said there could be no real revolution or change without violence: "...there's no such thing as a nonviolent revolution, the only kind of revolution that is nonviolent is the Negro revolution. The only revolution based on loving your enemies is the Negro revolution. The only revolution in which the goal is a desegregated lunch counter, a desegregated theater, a desegregated park, and a desegregated public toilet; you can sit down next to white folks on the toilet! That's no revolution."

Revolution or not, Mississippi exploded with violence one night in September 1962. An African American named James Meredith, had 9 years of military service behind him and had taken 12 college courses. He wanted to transfer to the very old, all-white University of Mississippi. The University of Mississippi was a symbol of the culture and traditions of the white South. Segregation was at its strongest there. The governor of Mississippi, Ross Barnett himself, stopped Meredith from signing up for classes there. President John F. Kennedy had to step in. He sent in his own marshals to make sure Meredith was admitted into the university. That night 160 marshals were in-

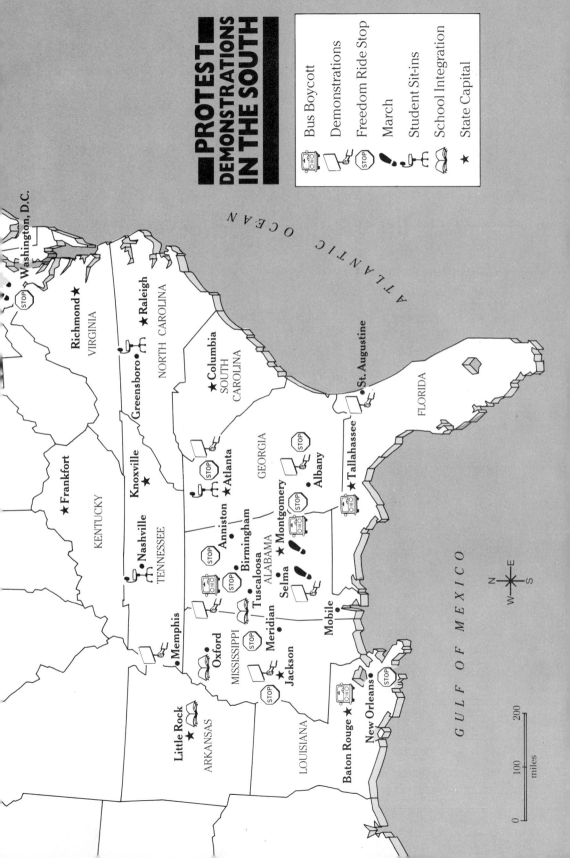

PROTEST DEMONSTRATIONS IN THE SOUTH

Bus Boycott
Demonstrations
Freedom Ride Stop
March
Student Sit-ins
School Integration
★ State Capital

Washington, D.C.

Richmond ★
VIRGINIA

Greensboro ● ★ Raleigh
NORTH CAROLINA

Columbia
★ SOUTH
CAROLINA

Frankfort ★
KENTUCKY

Knoxville
★
Nashville ●
TENNESSEE

Anniston ●
Atlanta ★
GEORGIA

St. Augustine ●

FLORIDA

ATLANTIC OCEAN

Birmingham ●
ALABAMA

Tuscaloosa ●
Selma ★ Montgomery

Albany ●

★ Tallahassee

Memphis ●

Oxford ●
MISSISSIPPI

Meridian ●

Jackson ★

Mobile ●

GULF OF MEXICO

Little Rock ★
ARKANSAS

LOUISIANA

Baton Rouge ★
New Orleans ●

N
W E
S

0   100   200
miles

jured, 28 marshals were shot, and two men lay dead. Here was some violence, people told Malcolm—surely this was change.

"Sir," Malcolm said during a radio talk show, "one little black man going to a school in Mississippi in no way compensates [makes up] for the fact that a million black people don't even get to the grade-school level in Mississippi." For Malcolm, these events didn't mean anything compared with the work that was still to be done.

But the violence grew worse. Martin Luther King, Jr., had chosen Birmingham as the next Albany. This time they were determined to win. Birmingham, Alabama, was one of the most segregated cities in the South. In 1962, the city closed 68 parks, 38 playgrounds, 6 swimming pools, and 4 golf courses to avoid a national court order telling the city to integrate its public places.

The supporters of the civil rights movement were determined to demonstrate in Birmingham until all the jails were filled. By May 6, 1963, more than 2,000 people had been jailed—including Dr. King. Theophilus Eugene "Bull" Connor, who was the head of the police department and a true believer in segregation, ordered fire hoses and police dogs to be turned on the young demonstrators. On TV news programs that day, the entire country watched as dogs ripped the clothes off children and other demonstrators. Fire hoses that were strong enough to rip the bark off trees swept people off their feet and slammed them into buildings.

Finally, the white people who owned most of the businesses in downtown Birmingham decided that something had to be done. It seemed that the African-American community was determined to march and stay away from their stores until segregation ended. The owners of these businesses were also afraid that their stores would be damaged. They knew that Bull Connor, who really ran the city, would never give in to the protestors. They decided to talk with Dr. King. By Monday,

May 10, the downtown stores had agreed to integrate and hire African Americans. The movement had won a major victory.

In Washington, President Kennedy had also been watching TV. He didn't want to see this kind of violence happen anywhere else in the United States. "We face," he announced, "a moral crisis as a country and as a people...I am therefore asking Congress to enact legislation giving all Americans the right to be served in facilities which are open to the public—hotels, restaurants, theaters, retail stores and similar establishments...." On June 19, this new civil rights bill was presented to Congress by the president. If passed, it would make segregation everywhere in the United States illegal.

The promise of new laws, however, didn't stop the violence in the South. On June 12, a popular director of the NAACP, Medgar Evers, was shot and killed. Police and rioters began to battle in the streets. Finally, in September, someone threw a bomb into a black church in Birmingham and killed four little girls. Malcolm had had enough. In November 1963, at a rally at the King Solomon Baptist Church in Detroit, he expressed his anger:

"As long as the white man sent you to Korea, you bled. He sent you to Germany, you bled. He sent you to the South Pacific to fight the Japanese, you bled. You bleed for white people, but when it comes to seeing your own churches being bombed and little black girls [being] murdered, you haven't got any blood. You bleed when the white man says bleed; you bite when the white man says bite; and you bark when the white man says bark...."

Malcolm believed that people had a right to defend themselves. This was even written in the U.S. Constitution. He hated to see his people being hurt this way. "Be patient, be peaceful, be Christian," said the whites. But Malcolm wanted African Americans everywhere to stand up and defend themselves. He pointed to all the countries in Africa that were winning their independence, building their own nations, taking positions of power in their own government, and sending white people away. It was exactly what Marcus Garvey had been trying to organize all those years ago. Malcolm saw no reason why African Americans couldn't build their own nation, one that was separate from the whites.

"Tell it like it is" the crowd shouted to Malcolm, urging him on. But he needed no encouragement. Fire was in his words that night, especially when he began talking about the so-called African-American leaders of the South. He was talking about Martin Luther King, Jr., more than anyone:

"Just as the slave master of that day used Tom . . . the same old slave master today has Negroes who are nothing but modern Uncle Toms, twentieth-century Uncle Toms, to keep you and me in check, to keep us under control, keep us passive and peaceful and nonviolent. That's Tom making you nonviolent. It's like when you go to the dentist, and the man's going to take your tooth. You're going to fight him when he starts pulling. So he squirts some stuff in your jaw called novocaine, to make you think they're not doing anything to you. So you sit there and because you've got all of that novocaine in your jaw, you suffer—peacefully. Blood running all down your jaw, and you don't know what's happening. Because someone has taught you to suffer—peacefully. . . ."

He took a breath, and then said quietly: "There is nothing in our book, the Koran, that teaches us to suffer peacefully. Our religion teaches us to be intelligent. Be peaceful, be courteous, obey the law, respect everyone; but if someone puts a hand on you," he thundered, "send him to the cemetery!" The crowd roared back its approval. No one could be as defiant as Malcolm X.

Malcolm finished by talking about the March on Washington. In June 1963, a quarter of a million blacks and whites had come from all over the country to march on the Capitol. They wanted to show their strength and determination to the world. They wanted to make sure that the civil rights bill proposed by President Kennedy was passed in Congress.

Malcolm called it the "farce on Washington." He spoke of how the leaders had been given white money, and how they had been promised more after the march. As a result, Malcolm said, the march became nothing but a circus and a picnic. "[The black leaders] controlled it so tight, they told those Negroes what time to hit town, how to come, where to stop, what signs to carry, what song to sing, what speech they could make, and what speech they couldn't make; and then told them to get out of town by sundown."

Most people believed that Malcolm was wrong about the March on Washington. One of the most moving moments the nation ever experienced was when Dr. King delivered his famous "I Have a Dream" speech there. It was a day of hope. With the recent changes, and with Congress being pressured to pass the new civil rights bill, many people felt that Dr. King's message of love and nonviolence would bring freedom to everyone.

In fact, Malcolm was trapped. He had been watching the battle in the South. He had seen people getting hurt and beaten. Malcolm, the great warrior, was being called to battle. The streets were running with blood. But there was nothing he could do. The Nation of Islam wanted to have nothing to do with the civil rights movement in the South. Mr. Muhammad wouldn't let him join in.

Malcolm's frustration grew. He knew what they were saying on the streets: "Those Muslims sure talk tough, but I've never seen them do anything. It's King's people who are doing all the fighting." Although Malcolm was unhappy that the Nation of Islam wasn't taking some kind of action, he had no intention of leaving. It was his home. It was the house he had built for himself. But Malcolm would soon learn that there were even bigger and stronger houses.

11 LOCKED OUT

66 I do not pretend to be a divine man," he said. "...I am not educated, nor am I an expert in any particular field. But I am sincere, and my sincerity [is] my credentials. 99

MALCOLM X, Park Sheraton Hotel press conference, March 12, 1964

66Minister Malcolm is trying to take over the Nation...Malcolm is trying to take credit for Mr. Muhammad's teachings...Malcolm likes playing coast-to-coast Mr. Big Shot." The rumors began when Mr. Muhammad left Chicago and moved to Arizona in 1961. Malcolm knew it would happen. Even Mr. Muhammad had told him so. Non-Muslims accused Malcolm of making "a pile of money." The truth was that Malcolm accepted only enough money for his family to live on. He and Betty had had a big argument about this. She wanted him to bring home a little extra and begin saving some money for their children. But Malcolm wouldn't do it.

Maybe he *was* doing too many things, Malcolm thought to himself. By 1963, he had begun to turn down interviews and radio shows. When he did speak in public, every other sentence mentioned "the honorable Mr. Muhammad." When reporters took photographs of Malcolm, he would immediately give them a photograph of the Messenger and ask them to use that instead. He even stopped some of his New York Muslim brothers from going out and setting up new temples. He knew they would be accused of doing it for Malcolm and not for Mr. Muhammad.

In spite of the ugly rumors, it seemed that Mr. Muhammad had more faith in Malcolm now than ever. In late 1963, at a rally in Philadelphia, Mr. Muhammad announced that Malcolm had been made the first national minister for the Nation of Islam. Malcolm rejoiced. Of course Mr. Muhammad believes in me! he must have thought to himself. But he couldn't have been more mistaken.

There were other rumors in the Nation of Islam that year. These weren't about Malcolm, though. They were about the Messenger himself. And these rumors had been going around much longer than the ones about Malcolm. They had begun as far back as 1955.

Some people said that the Messenger had been having sexual relations with some of his personal secretaries. Some of them had even had his children, people claimed. Malcolm refused to listen. But by late 1962, members were leaving the Chicago temple because of the rumors. Malcolm decided that he had to find out for himself.

He found the secretaries. They had been banned from the Nation of Islam by Mr. Muhammad, and no Muslims were allowed to talk to them. Malcolm broke that rule. He was rewarded with some painful news. Not only did they tell him that the rumors were true, but they also told him something much more disturbing. Mr. Muhammad had told his secretaries that

Malcolm was the best and greatest minister he had ever had. But someday he believed Malcolm would leave and turn against him. Mr. Muhammad said that Malcolm was dangerous.

Malcolm was stunned. In April 1963, he flew out to Arizona to ask Mr. Muhammad about the rumors. The Messenger took Malcolm outside and they started walking by the swimming pool. Malcolm found the courage to tell Mr. Muhammad about the poison being spread about him. Mr. Muhammad didn't deny the rumors. Instead, he said that it was written down a long time ago that this would happen.

Malcolm's world was shattered. Another house came tumbling down. He had thought that this house was stronger than any he had ever built before. His faith in the Messenger and the entire Nation of Islam was suddenly ripped from under him. He was numb, but he didn't stop working. He tried to prepare his ministers in Harlem in case the story reached the newspapers. He was amazed at how many ministers already knew.

The Chicago headquarters of the Nation of Islam looked at Malcolm's "preparation" in another way. Muslims there accused Malcolm of spreading the rumors even further. "I never dreamed that they would make it appear that I was throwing gasoline on the fire instead of water. I never dreamed that they were going to make it appear that instead of [protecting] against the epidemic, I had started it," Malcolm said.

On November 22, 1963, in Dallas, Texas, President John F. Kennedy was shot dead. Mr. Muhammad told all of his ministers not to say anything at all about the event. Three days later, Malcolm was at a rally in Harlem. During the question-and-answer period after the speech, Malcolm was asked what he thought about the death of President Kennedy. Malcolm forgot all about Mr. Muhammad's instructions. He just blurted out what he felt. "It's a case of the chickens coming home to roost," he said. His audience cheered and laughed. Then he added, "Being an old farm boy myself, chickens coming home to roost never did make me sad; they've always made me glad."

President John F. Kennedy and his wife, Jacqueline, seconds before he is gunned down in Dallas.

That fiery tongue of Malcolm's had gotten the better of him this time. He should have known that most whites wouldn't understand what he meant. He was really saying that there was so much hate in the United States that the ill will of whites would come back and haunt them. He wasn't saying that the president was a bad person. He was saying that his death was a result of a society that no longer cared properly for human beings. Most of the press—the newspapers and magazines, radio and TV people—didn't see it that way. They told the public that Malcolm had said the president got what was coming to him. Malcolm didn't get a chance to defend himself. Mr. Muhammad immediately silenced him for 90 days. This meant Malcolm could go on running his temples, but he was forbidden to speak in public for three months.

Malcolm X's remark wasn't the real reason he was silenced, though. This was just the excuse Mr. Muhammad and the Chicago headquarters of the Nation of Islam had been waiting for. They wanted to get him out, and he had given them the perfect opportunity.

Malcolm regretted what he'd said and told a journalist, "I should have kept my big mouth shut." Newspapers and magazines from all over the world called Malcolm, but he kept quiet. All he said was that he respected Mr. Muhammad's decision and that he expected to be talking again after the 90 days were over. But the other ministers in Chicago who were running the Nation of Islam shut Malcolm out and stopped him from teaching in his own temple. They said that he had rebelled against Mr. Muhammad. They began spreading rumors about things Malcolm had never done.

Malcolm couldn't believe what was happening: "I was in a state of emotional shock. I was like someone who for twelve years had had an inseparable, beautiful marriage—and then suddenly one morning at breakfast the marriage partner had thrust across the table some divorce papers...I felt as though something in *nature* had failed, like the sun, or the stars."

Muhammad Ali, the famous boxer, rescued Malcolm. They had met a year earlier and were good friends. In fact, Muhammad (who was then known as Cassius Clay) was about to become a member of the Nation of Islam. Malcolm had been guiding and teaching him. Muhammad Ali decided to give Malcolm and his family a sixth wedding anniversary present. He asked them to go on a vacation to Miami. There he was training to fight the world heavyweight champion, Sonny Liston. Malcolm agreed right away. It was a chance to escape from all his troubles and to think things out.

Florida was the first vacation Malcolm and Betty had ever had. By now they had three daughters: Attallah the oldest, Qubilah, who had been born on Christmas Day in 1960, and Ilyasah, who was one and a half. (Another daughter, Amilah, would be born the following year.) It was good to spend time with them—time he never seemed to have back in New York.

With the 90 days coming to an end, Malcolm begged the Nation of Islam to let him back in. His pleas fell on deaf ears. The doors to the house that he had lived in for so long were

Muhammad Ali, called Cassius Clay until he found Islam, beats Sonny Liston in their rematch.

suddenly shut in his face. He was out in the cold. Malcolm knew that it was the jealous ministers in Chicago who had poisoned the Messenger's mind against him.

Malcolm realized that he was on his own. He also realized that he had been given an opportunity to get more involved in the freedom struggle. He knew he couldn't join one of the civil rights organizations in the South. He still believed in the teachings of the Nation of Islam. He still believed in the building of a black nation and in separation rather than integration. He also believed that people could use one kind of violence to defend themselves against another kind of violence.

Malcolm also realized that he had a following all over the world. He understood that many people in the United States, of all different sorts of religions, wanted him to lead them. He also knew that he understood the anger and poverty of the black people in the northern cities better than any of the civil rights leaders. He knew how they thought and the language they used.

Things began to seem a little brighter and clearer for Malcolm. He knew there was only one road he could travel. "In the end I reasoned that the decision already had been made for me," he said. "The ghetto masses already had entrusted me with an image of leadership among them...I felt a challenge to plan, and build, an organization that could help to cure the black man in North America of the sickness which has kept him under the white man's heel."

On March 12, 1964, Malcolm called a press conference at the Park Sheraton Hotel in New York. He announced that he was still a Muslim and still believed in Mr. Muhammad. He said that the problems they had had were due to "internal differences [arguments among members of the group]" that had forced him out. He admitted that he hadn't left of his own free will.

Malcolm said he had decided to continue fighting outside the Nation of Islam. Mr. Muhammad's plan of total separation back to Africa was now a "long-range program," he explained. In the meantime, there was work to be done to feed, house, and get jobs for African Americans suffering right here and now. He called on the other civil rights leaders to join him: "The problem facing our people here in America is bigger than all the other personal or organizational differences. Therefore, as leaders, we must stop worrying about the threat that we seem to think we pose to each other's personal prestige, and concentrate our united efforts toward solving the unending hurt that is being done daily to our people here in America."

He finished the conference by announcing plans for his own new temple in New York. It would be called Muslim Mosque, Inc. It would be organized "in such manner to provide for the active participation of all Negroes in our political, economic, and social programs, despite their religious or non-religious beliefs," Malcolm said.

In many ways, Malcolm still didn't know how things would turn out. He hadn't really been specific about what the organization would do or how it would do it. He had simply made it known that he wasn't going to sit on the sidelines anymore and let the civil rights movement march past him. He wanted to get involved.

The Nation of Islam answered Malcolm's "declaration of independence" by sending him a letter. In it they asked for Malcolm's home in Queens to be turned over to them. The Nation of Islam had given Malcolm and his family the house to live in, but they had never put the ownership into his name. Now they wanted it back. Malcolm saw this as a sign of war.

The other leaders of the civil rights movement did little to respond to Malcolm. There was still a lot of mistrust and jealousy. Few of them had ever met or talked with Malcolm. Perhaps they were frightened that he would make them look like fools with his sharp tongue if they debated him in public. More importantly, they still disagreed on such basic questions as integration and the use of violence.

By now the Freedom Summer of 1964 was gaining strength in Mississippi. This was a big campaign to register African Americans to vote in the election for president that was coming up. Malcolm agreed that this was an important step in the right direction. He realized that black people could really make a difference in the government if they all got out and voted. After all, there were 22 million of them in the United States.

But before Malcolm set up a program of his own, there was something very important he had to do—something he had been wanting to do for many years. He decided to go to Mecca.

12 OMOWALE ("THE SON WHO HAS COME HOME")

> **❝ I think that the pilgrimage to Mecca broadened my scope probably more in twelve days than my previous experience during my thirty-nine years on this earth. ❞**
>
> MALCOLM X, *The Barry Gray Show*, WMCA, July 11, 1964

The religion of Islam as it was practiced all over the world wasn't the same as the religion that Mr. Muhammad was teaching. Malcolm had known this for a long time, but he had chosen to ignore it. To continue within the Nation of Islam, you *had* to ignore it. But he had been urged by many of his friends to discover the true religion of Islam for himself. He decided to make what is called a pilgrimage, a trip to a holy place to gain spiritual strength and understanding.

Telling almost no one, Malcolm left the United States on April 13, 1964, and flew to Cairo in Egypt. He spent two days sight-seeing there. He had been to Africa very briefly before for Mr. Muhammad, but he had hardly seen anything. In Egypt, he saw the future of Africa: developed, industrial countries with dams, factories, and railways. Then he left for the pilgrimage to Mecca.

At the airport in Cairo, people from all over Africa were gathering for the flight to Saudi Arabia. Malcolm began to get an idea of how many millions of Muslims there were in the world. He left all of his luggage in Cairo. For the pilgrimage, all you needed was faith. Everything else must be left behind. Malcolm and some of the other pilgrims changed into the simple clothes of a pilgrim—two white pieces of cloth. One was wrapped around the waist, and the other was slung over the shoulder. He felt a little awkward standing there. Not many of the people spoke English. Everything was so different! There was no doubt that this tall, quiet man from Harlem was a little frightened.

Malcolm discovered one thing that made him rejoice. "Packed in the plane were white, black, brown, red, and yellow people, blue eyes and blond hair, and my kinky red hair—all together, brothers!" he said. For the first time, he knew what it was like to be in a place where it didn't matter what color you were or how different you seemed.

Mecca is a holy city in Saudi Arabia. It is where the Prophet Muhammad lies buried. It is the heart of the Islamic world. It is where Islam began. If they are able to, all Muslims must make the pilgrimage to Mecca at least once in their life. This is called the hajj. The plane Malcolm was on landed at Jidda, 40 miles from Mecca. Jidda is a sort of religious customs post. This is where officials check to make sure you're a Muslim. No non-Muslim is allowed inside the city walls of Mecca. Malcolm was told to wait. The officials weren't used to Muslims from the United States. He would have to go before a special court. They would judge whether he was truly a Muslim. The court wouldn't be open again for another two days. He would have to wait at the airport.

Malcolm was taken to another building in the airport where others were also waiting to be allowed to go to Mecca. He stood there nervous and afraid, lonely and lost. He had no food. He couldn't talk to people because they didn't speak English. He couldn't pray like them because his knees and ankles wouldn't bend that far. If Mr. Muhammad didn't teach us how to pray properly, he thought, what else have we been doing wrong? He was worried that he wouldn't be accepted as a true Muslim. Malcolm tried to take his mind off things by watching all the different people around him. "I don't believe that motion picture cameras ever filmed a human [picture] more colorful than my eyes took in ... Chinese, Indonesians, Afghanistanians ... many ... still wore their national dress. It was like pages out of the *National Geographic* magazine," he said.

Then Malcolm had an idea. He had been given a telephone number in Jidda to call if he needed any help. He persuaded someone to call for him. Within a short while, a man named Dr. Omar Azzam arrived at the airport. Dr. Azzam and his father were very kind to Malcolm. Back at their home in Jidda, they scolded him. They said he should have called them earlier. Malcolm discovered that the Azzam family was one of the most important families in Saudi Arabia. They were even related to the ruler of Saudi Arabia himself, Prince Faisal. They were also white—at least that's what they would be considered in the United States. Malcolm was given their suite at a big Jidda hotel to stay in. He lay awake all night with new thoughts spinning around in his head.

"I am going to tell you that I had never been so honored in my life, nor had I ever received such true [friendship] ... I was speechless at the man's attitude, and at my own physical feeling of no difference between us as human beings," Malcolm wrote later. "That morning was when I first began to [think differently] about the 'white man.' It was when I first began to [see] that 'white man,' as commonly used, means color of skin only [second]; [first] it described attitudes and actions. In America, 'white man' meant specific attitudes and actions toward the black man, and toward all other non-white men."

The Azzam family taught Malcolm about the real history of the Muslims. They told him that the descendants of the Prophet Muhammad were both black and white. They also helped Malcolm get everything sorted out with the holy court. He was recognized as a true believer and approved for the hajj pilgrimage. The Azzam family had told Prince Faisal all about Malcolm, and the prince sent one of his cars to drive Malcolm to Mecca. How Malcolm's luck had changed since that first day at the airport in Jidda.

To complete the pilgrimage to Mecca, Malcolm had to perform some exercises that were hundreds of years old. He circled the holy building called the Kaaba seven times. He fell face-down on the ground as he declared his faith and belief in Allah. He drank from the well of Zem Zem. He ran seven times between the hills of Mount Al-Safa and Mount Al-Marwah. And he recited special prayers in the old city of Mina and on Mount Arafat.

This was true Islam, a religion in which people live together in peace no matter what their color. Malcolm saw this in practice. He watched people of many different colors praying, talking, and laughing together. There was no distrust or hatred here as there was back home. He felt liberated. Malcolm tried to put his thoughts down into long letters that he sent home to Betty and his closest friends:

"Never have I witnessed such sincere hospitality and the overwhelming spirit of true brotherhood as is practiced by people of all colors and races here in this Ancient Holy Land. . . . For the past week, I have been utterly speechless and spellbound by the graciousness I see displayed all around me by people *of all colors*. . . . You may be shocked by these words coming from me.

Muslims Around the World

A Muslim is a person who believes in Islam. Islam is one of the world's largest religions. Islam was begun in 622 A.D. by Muhammad, who lived in the cities of Medina and Mecca in Arabia. After he died, Islam spread throughout the world. Muslims consider Muhammad to be the last in a long line of messengers from Allah to people on earth. Other messengers have been Adam, Abraham, Moses, and Jesus. Muslims believe Muhammad was the most important and last of the prophets.

There are nearly one billion Muslims in the world. They live mostly in Indonesia, the Middle East, North Africa, Bangladesh, and Pakistan. There are many different groups of Muslims. The two biggest groups are called Sunni and Shiite. There are about five million Muslims in the United States today.

Muslims believe in one, all-powerful God whom they call Allah. Muslims believe there is a heaven and hell. They also have a holy book called the Koran. Muslims are not allowed to eat pork, drink alcohol, or gamble. They pray together, five times a day. Their houses of worship are called mosques. Muslims consider it a religious duty to give charity. They try to make the pilgrimage to Mecca at least once in their lives.

Chinese Muslims during prayers at the Grand Mosque in Xining, China.

Every year millions of Muslim pilgrims make the journey to Mecca in Saudi Arabia.

Muslim women in a Brooklyn, New York, mosque kneel facing east to pray.

But on this pilgrimage, what I have seen, and experienced, has forced me to *re-arrange* much of my thought-patterns previously held, and to *toss aside* some of my previous conclusions...."

Malcolm's entire life was about learning and changing. He now realized that *some* white people could be truly friendly. He now understood that word *white* in the United States really described someone's mind more than the color of his or her skin.

Malcolm X with Prince Faisal in Saudi Arabia.

Malcolm had known that his opinion about all whites being the devil wasn't quite right. He had been friendly with some whites and even respected some of them. But here in Mecca, he saw for the first time that it was wrong to judge anybody by the color of his or her skin. It was the *system* that should be blamed. It was the white history of slavery that should be blamed. It was the *attitudes* of some whites that should be blamed. If only they could all unite under Islam, he thought, then there would be no color problem in the United States.

Malcolm was now El Hajj Malik El Shabazz. He had completed the pilgrimage and taken on his true Muslim identity. This meant that he had to take a new name once again, though he continued to use Malcolm X as well.

Before he left Mecca, Malcolm X was a guest of state of Saudi Arabian Prince Faisal. Then Malcolm decided to visit Africa. If he could unite the people of Africa with his people back home, they could share in the struggle and give one another strength. He wasn't sure how to do this, or even whether they would help. He believed a link with Africa would give African Americans a link with their past—a link that could give them their identity. And with this identity would come pride. Malcolm never doubted this.

In Nigeria and elsewhere, Malcolm told the Africans about their black brothers and sisters in the United States. He told them that the American government had been spreading news about the progress in the United States. They were talking about the civil rights bill that President Kennedy had proposed. Malcolm felt these were lies. It wasn't real progress. Nothing would change the misery of his brothers and sisters in the United States until something much more important changed. He believed that this wouldn't happen until Africans all over the world united to help and support one another.

Malcolm could hardly believe how warmly he was greeted and accepted. Everyone seemed to know who he was. He was on television, on the radio, and found himself speaking before groups of people everywhere. He also met many important African and foreign diplomats and politicians. The Nigerian students even gave him a new name, "Omowale," which means "the son who has come home."

In Africa, Malcolm felt he had come home—after 400 years. Everywhere he went he wanted to slow down—to look, to smell, to *feel* Africa. In Nigeria, Senegal, Liberia, Morocco, Algeria, and especially Ghana, the Africans responded to his call for help. But it wasn't easy for them. They hoped to get money from the United States to help their young nations grow. They didn't want to do anything that would upset the United States. But they did listen to Malcolm.

On May 21, two days after his thirty-ninth birthday, Malcolm arrived at John F. Kennedy International Airport in New York City. In Ghana he had begun thinking about a new organization. He couldn't wait to get it started in America. He was eager to tell everyone what he had discovered while he was gone. He would have to explain sooner than he thought.

HUMAN RIGHTS, NOT CIVIL RIGHTS

> *❝ The greatest mistake of the movement has been trying to organize a sleeping people around specific goals. You have to wake the people up first then you'll get action."*
>
> *"Wake them up to their exploitation?"*
>
> *"No, to their humanity, to their own worth, and to their heritage. ❞*

MALCOLM X, in conversation with Marlene Nadle of the *Village Voice*

Flashbulbs burst and blinded Malcolm X. Questions were shouted across the room. People with cameras pushed and shoved one another to get a better glimpse. Malcolm X was back!

The press had been waiting for him at the airport. At first Malcolm thought there was a celebrity on the plane. But he was the one the press wanted. The questions came quickly. What about all these changes? Has your attitude toward white people changed? Whom did you meet in Africa? Have you been organizing the violence in Harlem?

Malcolm answered all their questions that day. He told them that his outlook had been broadened. Many of them were white. They wanted to hear him say that white people weren't devils. By nature, Malcolm answered, they weren't. But by their actions, white people in the United States were still the devils he had always thought they were.

There had already been some violence in Harlem. African Americans there had talked about getting guns and organizing themselves into rifle clubs. The press asked Malcolm about that. "Self-defense," Malcolm said. "There's nothing wrong with that."

Five weeks later, Malcolm announced the details of his new organization. It would be called the Organization of Afro-American Unity (OAAU). To kick things off, Malcolm arranged a big rally in a large hall called the Audubon Ballroom in Harlem. The rally took place on June 28, 1964. That day the big, long hall was filled. People were eager to hear Malcolm's news.

Malcolm didn't want his new organization to be religious. He was still a very religious man, but he didn't want to divide his people in any way—not even by religious differences. He wanted them to know that this was an organization for *all* African Americans. He wasn't just talking about all the African Americans in Harlem. He meant all the people of African descent in the Western Hemisphere.

Malcolm had a lot to say about self-defense. For a long time the press had unfairly described him as someone who proposed violence just for the sake of violence. But Malcolm made it clear that if violence was needed to stop the violence of racism, then his people would be ready to do "whatever is necessary." He felt that if the government wasn't able or willing to protect African Americans, they should take up arms and protect themselves. Malcolm felt strongly that they couldn't use nonviolence to fight violence. As soon as whites stopped beating up his people, setting dogs on them, murdering them, and turning fire hoses on them, then he would be willing to be nonviolent.

Many whites, and some blacks, believed Malcolm was only spreading more hate. But Malcolm knew that he was inspiring blacks with the confidence and courage they needed to defy authority and change things. "I won't permit you to call it hate. Let's say I'm going to create an awareness of what has been done to them. This awareness will produce an abundance of energy, both negative and positive, that can then be channeled constructively," he told a reporter in New York.

At the rally at the Audubon Ballroom that night, Malcolm also stressed how important education was. "It is the means to help our children and our people rediscover their identity and thereby increase their self-respect," he said. "When we send our children to school in this country they learn nothing about us other than that we used to be cotton pickers...Why, your grandfather was Nat Turner; your grandfather was Hannibal. Your grandfather was some of the greatest black people who walked on this earth. It was your grandfather's hands who forged civilization and it was your grandmother's hands who rocked the cradle of civilization. But the textbooks tell our children nothing about the great contributions of Afro-Americans to the growth and development of this country!" shouted Malcolm.

Malcolm had great plans for the OAAU. He talked about neighborhoods getting rid of drugs and crime. He talked about African Americans and the need "to unbrainwash an entire people." Malcolm told his people that the problem in the United States was something that Uncle Sam would never solve. He told them that they needed to "internationalize" their struggle—

get help and sympathy from other countries all over the world. He said it was wrong to see this as a matter of civil rights. It was more a question of human rights! What African Americans wanted was something that every human being had a right to have. Malcolm wanted to introduce a proposal in the United Nations that said the United States wasn't respecting the human rights of its African-American people.

Malcolm wanted the new OAAU to start youth groups, speakers programs, a new newspaper, and political and economic programs. He wanted some positive action that would wake his people up. He wanted to change society, not just integrate it. Malcolm believed this change would not come from whites. It would have to come from blacks themselves.

As the summer of 1964 moved on, the white press called Malcolm all sorts of names in the newspapers for threatening to use violence. Malcolm wasn't saying violence was a good thing. He pointed out that white people had used violence against people of other color for centuries, and that whites in the United States were still using violence. Even the colonies had used violence to free themselves from England, he pointed out. Suddenly, Malcolm showed, violence wasn't allowed because African Americans were threatening to use it for their own protection and self-defense!

It was only when Malcolm talked about violence that the white press printed anything he said. It was only when he talked about hate that they listened. It was only when he criticized the other movement—the civil rights movement in the South—that they put him on TV. This was the portrait they drew of Malcolm across the country. Many people never heard him talk about pride, human rights, or self-defense. They didn't hear his plans for social change. "They were looking for sensationalism, for something that would sell papers, and I gave it to them," Malcolm explained. "If they had asked probing intelligent questions, they would have gotten different answers."

Malcolm was also beginning to fear for his life. Ever since he had left the Nation of Islam, he had heard rumors of threats to his life. He kept a shotgun at home to protect his family. He let everyone know that he was ready to shoot whoever tried to get into the house. He also applied for a permit to carry a pistol.

The Nation of Islam continued to try to throw Malcolm and his family out of their house in Queens. Malcolm had very little to leave his family in case he died. Now even the house they lived in was being taken away from them. Malcolm was upset. He had never wanted to leave the Nation of Islam. They had pushed him out. Now that he was shaping a much more important movement, they wanted to get back at him. Well, they had asked for it, and Malcolm gave it to them! He began to talk openly about the rumors concerning Mr. Muhammad. He began to collect sworn statements from the women who had accused Mr. Muhammad of being the father of their children. Things only got worse between the two groups.

In June 1964, some of Malcolm's followers were in Boston heading out toward the airport. In the middle of a tunnel, two cars forced them to stop. A group of men jumped out and started toward the car with knives, shouting, "We're going to kill the . . . ." But one of Malcolm's men pulled out a shotgun and frightened them off. Fortunately, Malcolm wasn't there.

In July, Malcolm returned to Africa. This time he was away for 18 weeks. He traveled much more than he had during his first visit. He met with religious and political leaders from many different countries—including Egypt, Tanzania, Nigeria, Ghana, Guinea, Kenya, and Uganda. This trip was also more formal than the first one had been. He was greeted as if he were a member of another government. He was granted the respect and attention that visiting heads of state usually get.

Some of these leaders asked Malcolm about the new civil rights bill that had finally been signed into law on July 9. Malcolm made his position clear. This was no advance for their black brothers and sisters in America, he told them. There would be no advance until they brought pressure on the United States government through the United Nations.

At the conference for the Organization of African Unity in Cairo, the African nations had gathered for talks. Malcolm was there. Although he wasn't allowed to speak, he did get to hand out copies of a long letter he had written criticizing the United States. He had written, "Our problem is your problem. It is not a Negro problem, nor an American problem. This is a world problem; a problem for humanity. It is not a problem of civil rights but a problem of human rights."

Some people didn't think Malcolm had achieved much on his trip or with his letter. Some people believed he should have been at home working on his new organization. But at least Malcolm reminded the African people that the problem of their brothers and sisters in the United States wasn't over by a long way, despite what the U.S. government told them. At least he made them aware that there was a real racial problem in the United States. They wouldn't forget Malcolm X for a long time.

14

BOMBS AND GUNS

> **❝ The price of Freedom is death. ❞**
>
> **MALCOLM X, in a television interview**

❝Malcolm! We want Malcolm! Wait till Malcolm comes!" shouted the children as they ran through the burning streets of Harlem that night.

During Malcolm's absence, the summer of 1964 had become long, hot, and violent. On July 16, a school fight broke out in Harlem and a policeman shot and killed a 15-year-old boy. Harlem was like a pile of dry wood, and this was the match that sparked it off. Windows were smashed, stores were looted, buildings were set on fire. One person was killed, 140 were injured, and 500 were arrested. The anger wasn't just bottled up in Harlem either. Riots in Chicago, Philadelphia, and cities in New Jersey had followed. African Americans in the cities of the North understood what Malcolm was saying when he told them to defend themselves and stand up for their rights. Many of them were trapped in poverty and had very little to lose. What's more, Malcolm talked their language. He had grown up on the streets. He understood them, and they understood him.

In the South, Mississippi had also had its share of violence during the summer of 1964. Even before Malcolm left for Africa, three civil rights workers had disappeared in Mississippi. Two of them were white. They were involved in the program called Freedom Summer. After two months of searching, the bodies of the civil rights workers were discovered buried. They had been murdered.

The two organizations that were leading the project, the SNCC and CORE, had led their people into a war zone where their people were brutalized and murdered. By now many members of the SNCC and CORE weren't satisfied with how slowly things were changing in the South. They had begun to have their doubts about what integration would achieve. They were angry that it had taken the death of two white people to outrage the nation when blacks had been dying for so long. They were tired of nonviolence. Slowly but surely, Malcolm's ideas seemed to be making much more sense.

When Malcolm came back from Africa on November 24, 1964, the OAAU had almost fallen apart. The organization had no money, and its members couldn't agree on anything. They needed Malcolm's strong leadership and his clear voice.

Malcolm knew what was needed in the long run, but he didn't know which course of action would get him and his people there. All he could say was that he was "flexible": "I'm for the freedom of the 22 million Afro-Americans by any means necessary. *By any means necessary.* I'm for a society in which our people are recognized and respected as human beings.... So when you ask me where I'm headed, what can I say? I'm headed in any direction that will bring us some immediate results."

Malcolm knew that he could be killed for what he was saying.

"When I say by any means necessary, I mean it with all my heart, my mind and my soul," he said. "A black man should give his life to be free and he should also be willing to take the life of those who want to take his. When you really think like that, you don't live long."

The Fruit of Islam seemed to be wherever Malcolm was. If he gave a speech in Harlem or took a trip to Los Angeles or Chicago, they were there. They were trying to frighten him, and it was working. They were even attacking and shooting some of Malcolm's followers. In January 1965, Malcolm himself was attacked outside his home, but he managed to escape unhurt. A few days later in Los Angeles, two cars followed him for a while, then pulled up next to his car. Malcolm's people were frightened. This time they didn't have a gun. Malcolm pulled out a long walking cane that looked like a gun and scared them off. Malcolm flew on to Chicago, where he was kept under heavy guard by the Chicago police for three days. The Los Angeles police had called ahead to warn them that Malcolm X was being followed and could be killed at any time.

The police in Chicago and Los Angeles weren't the only ones who knew that Malcolm was in serious danger. BOSS (the Bureau of Special Services)—spies for the New York Police Department—knew this better than anyone. Along with the Central Intelligence Agency (CIA) and the Federal Bureau of Investigation (FBI), they had a thick file on Malcolm, reporting on everything he did. They had hidden microphones in his office so they could hear his conversations. Also, one of Malcolm's closest bodyguards turned out to be one of their spies. BOSS knew that relations between Malcolm and the Nation of Islam had reached a low point. Things had gotten so bad, in fact, that they were sure the Nation of Islam would soon try to kill him. During the last two weeks of Malcolm's life, the authorities in New York City offered him police protection three times. But Malcolm's life had been built on attacking the white government. He couldn't accept their protection. He refused.

Malcolm X and Martin Luther King, Jr., disagreed about the methods to use to fight racism.

SNCC invited Malcolm X to go to Selma, Alabama. He went there on February 4, 1965. This was one of the first signs that some of the southern organizations were becoming influenced by Malcolm's ideas. Dr. Martin Luther King, Jr., was in jail for nonviolent protesting at the time, but Malcolm X sat next to Dr. King's wife, Coretta Scott King, at the church where he spoke.

It was an important speech. Malcolm made it clear that other people who weren't as patient or as nonviolent as Dr. King would be ready to come down and change things. He didn't want to cause trouble for Dr. King, he had whispered to Coretta. He just wanted to help the movement by frightening white people with "the alternative."

Malcolm also traveled to England and France to give talks in February. The French government refused to let him into their country. They wouldn't explain why they did this. Malcolm began to wonder whether the United States government might have had something to do with this. He was back in New York on February 13.

That night Malcolm relived a terrible moment of his childhood. At about 2:30 A.M., a fire bomb crashed through the window, followed by another and then another. Within minutes, the house was filled with flames and smoke. Malcolm scrambled around to save his family. He managed to get all four daughters out safely, along with Betty, who was now pregnant with twins. They stood outside in the freezing cold, watching their home burn to the ground. On this night, Malcolm's thoughts must have turned to that other night 36 years ago when his parents had pulled him from their burning house.

Malcolm was angry because his family had been dragged into the fight. "They had better not harm my family," he fumed. "There are hunters; there are also the hunted." The Nation of Islam denied that they were responsible. They claimed that Malcolm had burned his own house for the sake of cheap publicity.

The house was destroyed, and Malcolm had never been able to afford fire insurance. He didn't know what to do. Betty and the children went to stay with friends. The next day he flew to Detroit for a meeting that he couldn't get out of, but he returned on Monday. He began canceling some of his future engagements. The following Friday, Malcolm made his last public speech at Columbia University in New York City.

"We are living in an era of Revolution," he preached, "and the revolt of the American Negro is part of that rebellion. It is incorrect to classify the revolt of the Negro as simply a racial conflict of black against white, or as a purely American problem. Rather, we are today seeing a global rebellion of slaves against slaveowners, the ones who are being taken advantage of against those who take advantage." Malcolm was now fighting for all people who were treated badly—black or white, yellow or brown.

The fire had forced Malcolm to think once again about the future of his family. On his return from Africa, he had promised never to go away again without taking Betty and the children with him. Now he made an appointment with his lawyer to make a will. The following Saturday, he went house hunting with Betty. They found a house on Long Island and wondered how they could raise the $4,000 they needed just to move in.

That afternoon Betty went back to their friend's house, and Malcolm drove into Manhattan. He checked into a single room in the Hilton Hotel. He needed to be alone to work things out. Malcolm was having serious doubts about who was really trying to kill him. In fact, that day he had told Alex Haley, the writer who was working with him on the story of his life, that he was going to stop blaming the Nation of Islam. Somehow, it just didn't make sense that the French government had refused to let him into the country.

The next morning Malcolm called Betty. He had changed his mind about her and the children staying away from the rally that afternoon. He wanted them there this time. By about two o'clock on the afternoon of February 21, 1965, Malcolm climbed the stairs to the small dressing room in the Audubon Ballroom. He had asked about eight guest speakers to appear, but none of them had come. Malcolm was tired and upset. He still hadn't recovered from the fire bombing.

"He was more tense than I'd ever seen him," said Benjamin Goodman, his right-hand man, "and I'd seen him for seven years. He just lost control of himself completely. I never saw him do that before."

By now the hall was filling with people. No one was searching the audience for weapons. Malcolm had ordered his men not to do this. It frightened people away, he said. When it was time to begin, Goodman went up onstage to introduce Malcolm as he had done so many times before. Malcolm appeared onstage, striding across to the speaker's stand.

Malcolm turned and looked out at his audience. He let them clap for a while. He looked out into their faces. Malcolm never got tired of hearing support from his people.

"*As-salaam-alaikum!*" shouted Malcolm with the Muslim greeting.

"*Wa-alaikum-salaam!*" they shouted back.

Suddenly, in the middle of the crowd, two people stood up and began shouting at each other. Malcolm's bodyguards moved into the crowd. Malcolm pleaded from the stage, "Stay cool, stay calm...."

Suddenly, right in front of Malcolm, a man with a sawed-off shotgun appeared.

"BOOM!" echoed the gun as the buckshot pellets ripped through the speaker's stand and hit Malcolm in the chest. "BOOM!" went the gun again as Malcolm toppled over backward, crashing through the empty chairs behind him and hitting the floor with a thud.

Two other men leapt out of the audience with guns and began firing into Malcolm. But the first shot had been enough. Malcolm lay there dying. Everyone was screaming and shouting, scrambling for cover. Betty had grabbed the children and was covering them with her body under a table.

One of Malcolm's men bent over his bloody body and tried to breathe life back into him. Betty ran over to her husband, screaming, "They're killing my husband, they're killing my husband." As some people tried to bring Malcolm back to life, others stood confused and shocked. No one could believe what had just happened. After a few minutes, a stretcher was brought onto the stage. Malcolm's body was rushed to the Columbia Presbyterian Medical Center, which was just across the street. The doctors began to work on Malcolm. They opened up his throat to allow him to breathe. They tried to get his heart beating again. They knew it was no use, but they tried anyway. After 15 minutes of intense work, they pulled a white sheet over his face.

El Hajj Malik El Shabazz, Malcolm X, Malcolm Little, was dead.

15 EPILOGUE

> *66 Dr. King wants the same thing I want: Freedom. 99*

MALCOLM X

No one knows who really killed Malcolm X. The police caught the people they thought had pulled the trigger. But they never found those who were thought to have put the guns into their hands. One man, Talmadge Hayer, was caught just outside the ballroom. He was rescued from the angry crowd by two policemen who happened to be driving past. The police arrested two other Muslims from the Nation of Islam. All of them were found guilty. All of them were sentenced to life in prison.

Not everybody believed that the whole truth came out at the trial. Hayer was the only one who admitted having killed Malcolm—too many people had seen him clearly. The other two claimed they were innocent. Hayer said they were telling the truth. But he never told anyone who helped him until 1977, when he began to talk again. This time he gave the names of the other people who had been involved. He confessed that he had been working for the Nation of Islam. He said that the murder was an act of revenge for Malcolm's "slander" against Mr. Muhammad. Despite Hayer's confession, the state of New York refused to reopen the case. It didn't believe what Hayer said.

There were other people who didn't believe Hayer's confession. They suspected that Malcolm's death was organized by the United States government. Malcolm was certainly beginning to cause embarrassment in the United Nations. He was also blamed for some of the violence in the northern cities. People still wonder why Malcolm wasn't allowed into France and why there was no police protection at the Audubon Ballroom on that fateful afternoon. Files released later by the FBI under the Freedom of Information Act suggested that the government was more heavily involved than most people imagined. An important memo was written in January 1969 to J. Edgar Hoover, the head of the FBI, from the bureau's Chicago office. The agents in Chicago boasted that they had made the fight between the Nation of Islam and Malcolm worse, thus directly contributing to his death. Other people believe that Harlem drug lords killed Malcolm because he was cleaning up the streets and helping addicts kick the habit. Years after Malcolm's death, many questions remain without answers.

For a week after his death, about 22,000 people viewed Malcolm's body at the Unity Funeral Home on Eighth Avenue in Harlem. There he lay, in a bronze and velvet coffin, looking calm and untroubled. A simple plate on the coffin read: "El Hajj Malik El Shabazz, May 19, 1925–Feb. 21, 1965."

On the Friday after Malcolm's death, an important-looking old man appeared at the funeral home. He had a long white beard, a forked walking stick, and was dressed in a turban and flowing white robes. It was Sheik Ahmed Hassoun. Sheik Hassoun had come over from Africa the year before to help Malcolm learn about the traditional Islamic religion and spread its teaching in the United States. Slowly and carefully, he and his assistants prepared Malcolm's body for burial in the traditional Muslim fashion. They removed Malcolm's Western clothing, washed his body in holy oil, and then draped him in seven white linen shrouds.

Malcolm's funeral was held the following day—on Saturday, February 27, 1965. His body was taken up to the church, the Faith Temple, Church of God in Christ, early that morning. More than 1,000 people managed to squeeze into the church that day. There were more than 6,000 outside on the streets. Harlem had never seen anything like this. Hundreds of police officers were present—on rooftops and out of sight, ready for any trouble. But there wasn't any.

Messages came from all over the world, especially Africa. But it was actor Ossie Davis who said it best:

"Here—at this final hour, in this quiet place, Harlem has come to bid farewell to one of its brightest hopes—extinguished now and gone from us forever. . . . Many will ask what Harlem finds to honor in this stormy, controversial and bold young captain—and we will smile. . . . They will say that he is of hate—a fanatic, a racist—who can only bring evil to the cause for which you struggle!

"And we will answer and say unto them: Did you ever talk to Brother Malcolm? Did you ever touch him, or have him smile at you? Did you ever really listen to him? Did he ever do a mean thing? Was he ever himself associated with violence or any public disturbance? For if you did you would know him. And if you knew him you would know why we must honor him: Malcolm was our manhood, our living black manhood! This was his meaning to his people. And, in honoring him, we honor the best in ourselves. . . . And we will know him then for what he

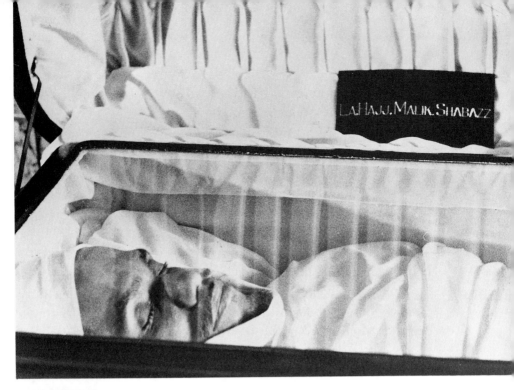

Malcolm X, African-American leader, before his burial.

was and is—a Prince—our own black shining Prince!—who didn't hesitate to die, because he loved us so."

Mrs. Betty Shabazz showed incredible strength at the time of her husband's murder. Their oldest daughter, Attallah, remembers those times: "Our mother kept our home strictly private, and she kept a very low profile, which immensely helped us. We knew she was grieving and that she was working very hard—we were just too little to realize how much of either." Mrs. Shabazz made the pilgrimage to Mecca "to put all the pieces of my life back together again." Seven months after her husband's death, she gave birth to twin girls—Malaak and Malikah. Now Mrs. Shabazz had six children to house and feed. She found herself in a situation not unlike Malcolm's mother, Louise Little, after Rev. Earl Little's death. Mrs. Shabazz went back to school and earned a doctorate in education from the University of Massachusetts. This allowed her to get better jobs and earn more money so that she could provide for her children. Back in New York, Dr. Shabazz began to teach health at Medgar Evers College. She has also traveled all over the country, lecturing about her experiences and talking about Malcolm: "He is the absolute best human being that I've ever had the pleasure to meet.... He introduced me to the world. This man expanded my narrow existence to a global view. He was an incredible man."

Malcolm's organization, the OAAU, was taken over by his half sister, Ella Collins, in Boston, but it failed to grow into the movement Malcolm had hoped it would be.

The Nation of Islam said they had nothing to do with the death of Malcolm. Mr. Muhammad claimed that Malcolm died as a result of the "violence" that he preached. Ten years later, in 1975, the Messenger himself died. His son, Wallace Muhammad, was left in charge of the Nation of Islam. But Wallace didn't agree with all of his father's beliefs. He began to reshape the Nation of Islam, making it more like the traditional Islam in the East. He allowed white people as well as black people to become members. He allowed members to enter politics or join the army—things his father would never have put up with. Wallace Muhammad even changed the name of the organization—first to the World Community of Islam in the West and later to the American Muslim Mission. In 1985, Wallace resigned as leader, telling local mosques, or temples, to organize themselves. During Wallace's leadership, many people became dissatisfied. Some left to form their own version of the Nation of Islam. The most well known and successful was an organization led by Minister Louis Farrakhan. He left the World Community of Islam in 1978 and guided his followers back to the strict teachings and beliefs of Mr. Muhammad. In 1990, membership was estimated at between 5,000 and 10,000 people.

The civil rights movement in the South struggled on. Selma, a place Malcolm had visited less than three weeks before his death, turned out to be one of the last major battlefields for the movement in the South. Selma was chosen by SNCC back in 1963 as an example of how local white governments prevented blacks from voting. Tough tests were required before they were allowed to register. This was truly unfair because many blacks in the South couldn't read. Offices to register were open for only two days a month in Selma. People who came to register had to wait for hours and were often frightened away by the local police.

A 26-year-old young man named Jimmy Lee Jackson died when the police shot him in the stomach. This incident roused Martin Luther King, Jr., and the SCLC to organize a march from Selma to the state capital of Alabama, Montgomery. The march was stopped twice by Governor George Wallace. The first time, tear gas and clubs were used by the state police on horseback to force the marchers to turn back. All over the country, people watched on TV as the police clubbed peaceful marchers on the Edmund Pettus Bridge. Finally, President Lyndon B. Johnson persuaded Governor George Wallace to let them march. On Sunday, March 21, the 54-mile march to Montgomery began. In all, 25,000 people had joined the march by the time it arrived in Montgomery. Selma, and the march, turned out to be the last major victory for the movement in the South. On August 6, 1965, the president signed the Voting Rights Act into law. This outlawed unfair rules that prevented people from registering to vote. African Americans were now in a position to have much more say in who was elected to local positions of power. Over the next few years, they would use that power all across the nation.

Dr. King battled on. Like Malcolm, his ideas changed and grew over the years. When the obvious barriers of segregation fell in the South, Dr. King moved on to attack more basic problems such as poverty and poor housing. He still believed the fight could remain nonviolent. He still believed that the good nature of human beings would win in the end. He was in the process of accomplishing more "far-reaching changes" for

As both a Muslim and an African-American leader, Malcolm X was completely dedicated to his work.

black people and organizing the poor people's March on Washington when his voice was silenced one fateful morning. On a balcony at the Lorraine Motel in Memphis, Tennessee, on April 4, 1968, Dr. Martin Luther King, Jr., was shot and killed. Like Malcolm, he was also 39 when he died.

Malcolm X was important to events of the 1960s and early 1970s in more ways than some people have ever understood. SNCC and CORE had begun to listen to Malcolm X while he was still alive. They ended up abandoning the goal of integration and the nonviolence as a way of reaching this goal. Under the leadership of Stokely Carmichael, who had listened to Malcolm X, SNCC began using the slogan "Black Power" to express its goals.

One group that owed a lot to the teachings of Malcolm was the Black Panthers. This was a political party set up in 1966, in California, by Bobby Seale and Huey Newton. Using Malcolm's message of self-defense, the Panthers armed themselves with guns and wore a uniform of army trousers, black leather jackets, and black berets as caps. They wanted to protect their community and their people against brutal acts by the police.

They followed the police wherever they went. Several times this ended in shootouts. California passed gun laws that forced the Panthers to lay down their arms. In the late 1960s, the Panthers began to work with white groups who agreed that the problem wasn't so much white against black, as rich against poor.

The cities of the North continued to express their anger and frustration in the only way they could be heard. In the summer of 1966 there were 43 riots, and in the first nine months of 1967 there were 164—with 2,000 people injured, 80 dead, and $664 million of damage. Segregation cast heavy chains of poverty around the African Americans of the northern cities; chains that seemed too heavy to break or shrug off. Malcolm's message and example led many people to reject the way things were and try to fight for something better. His love and humanity shone on many different groups of people during the 1960s and 1970s, leading them to stand up and challenge what they felt was unfair.

As the 20th century comes to a close, for many people the goals of integration still seem distant. But Malcolm's followers believe that more people will turn and listen to the words of Malcolm X. In listening and watching, they will discover a man who wasn't driven by hate but by love. They will find a man who spoke of violence only in the name of peace. They will find a gentle and loving father, as well as an angry prophet.

They will see how Malcolm untangled the chains of segregation and racism in the United States, chains that bound people's minds in a new kind of slavery. They will see how he tried to set his people, and oppressed people everywhere, free by giving them the courage to stand up and fight for what was rightfully theirs: their human rights.

They will learn that Malcolm X's voice was not silenced by the shotguns in the Audubon Ballroom.

Timetable of Events in the Life of Malcolm X

May 9, 1925	Born in Omaha, Nebraska
1940	Moves to Boston to live with half-sister, Ella Collins
1942	Moves to Harlem, New York City
1946	Begins seven-year prison term for robbery
1949	Becomes a member of Muslim Nation of Islam
1952	Released from prison
1953	Becomes assistant minister for the Detroit temple
1954	Becomes minister of Temple Number 7 in Harlem
1958	Marries Sister Betty Begins writing *Muhammad Speaks*
1959	Takes first trip to Middle East and Africa
1963	Becomes first national minister for Nation of Islam Nation of Islam silences Malcolm X
1964	Leaves Nation of Islam and starts Muslim Mosque, Inc. Makes pilgrimage to Mecca and second trip to Africa Changes name to El Hajj Malik El Shabazz Founds the OAAU
Feb. 21, 1965	Assassinated

SUGGESTED READING

*Adoff, Arnold. *Malcolm X*. New York: Crowell, 1970.

Branch, Taylor. *Parting the Waters: America in the King Years 1954–63*. New York: Simon and Schuster, 1988.

Breitman, George. *The Assassination of Malcolm X*. New York: Pathfinder Press, 1976.

*Dudley, Randall, and Margaret Burroughs, eds. *For Malcolm: Poems on The Life and The Death of Malcolm X*. New York: Broadside Press, 1973.

Epps, Archie, ed. *The Speeches of Malcolm X at Harvard*. New York: William Morrow, 1968.

Goldman, Peter. *The Death and Life of Malcolm X*. Chicago: University of Illinois Press, 1979.

Haley, Alex. *The Autobiography of Màlcolm X*. New York: Ballantine, 1988.

*Haskins, James. *The Picture Life of Malcolm X*. New York: Franklin Watts, 1975.

Lincoln, C. Eric. *Black Muslims in America*. Boston: Beacon, 1961.

Lomax, Louis E. *When the Word is Given: A Report on Elijah Muhammed, Malcolm X, and the Black Muslim World*. Cleveland: World, 1963.

Malcolm X. *By Any Means Necessary*. New York: Pathfinder Press, 1970.

Malcolm X. *Malcolm X on Afro-American History*. New York: Pathfinder Press, 1967.

Malcolm X. *Malcolm X Speaks*. New York: Grove Press, 1966.

Morris, Aldon. *The Origins of the Civil Rights Movement*. New York: The Free Press, 1984.

Perry, Bruce, ed. *Malcolm X: The Last Speeches*. New York: Pathfinder Press, 1989.

Rummel, Jack. *Malcolm X*. Los Angeles: Melrose Square Publishing, 1989.

*White, Florence Meiman. *Malcolm X: Black and Proud*.Champaign, IL:Garrard Publishing, 1975.

Williams, Juan. *Eyes on the Prize*. New York: Penguin, 1988.

---

*Readers of *Malcolm X: Another Side of the Movement* will find these books particularly readable.

SOURCES

BOOKS

Adoff, Arnold. *Malcolm X*. New York: Crowell, 1970.

Branch, Taylor. *Parting the Waters: America in the King Years 1954–63*. New York: Simon and Schuster, 1988.

Breitman, George. *The Assassination of Malcolm X*. New York: Pathfinder Press, 1976.

Breitman, George. *The Last Year of Malcolm X: The Evolution of a Revolutionary*. New York: Merit, 1987.

Brisbane, Robert. *Black Activisim: Racial Revolution in the United States*. Valley Forge, Pa.: Judson Press, 1974.

Curtis, Richard. *The Life of Malcolm X*. Philadelphia: Macrae Smith Company, 1971.

David, Lenwood G. *Malcolm X: A Selected Bibliography*. Westport, Conn.: Greenwood Press, 1984.

Epps, Archie, ed. *The Speeches of Malcolm X At Harvard*. New York: Morrow, 1968.

Farmer, James. *Lay Bare the Heart: An Autobiography of the Civil Rights Movement*. New York: Plume, 1985.

Floski, Harry A., and Warren Marr, eds. *The Negro Almanac: A Reference Work on the Afro-American*. New York: Bellweather Co., 1976.

Goldman, Peter. *The Death and Life of Malcolm X*. Chicago: University of Illinois Press, 1979.

Goldman, Peter. "Malcolm X: Witness for the Prosecution" in *Black Leaders of the Twentieth Century*, ed. John Hope Franklin and August Meier. Urbana: University of Illinois Press, 1982

Haley, Alex. *The Autobiography of Malcolm X*. New York: Ballantine, 1988.

Haskins, James. *The Picture Life of Malcolm X*. New York: Franklin Watts, 1975.

Lincoln, C. Eric. *Black Muslims in America*. Boston: Beacon, 1961.

Maglangbayan, Shawna. *Garvey, Lumumba and Malcolm: National Separatists*. Chicago: Third World Press, 1972.

Malcolm X. *By Any Means Necessary*. New York: Pathfinder Press, 1970.

Malcolm X. *Malcolm X on Afro-American History*. New York: Pathfinder Press, 1967.

Malcolm X. *Malcolm X Speaks*. New York: Grove Press, 1966.

Malcolm X Surveillance File, 1953–1971. Wilmington, Del.: Scholarly Resources, 1978.

Morris, Aldon. *The Origins of the Civil Rights Movement*. New York: The Free Press, 1984.

Perry, Bruce, ed. *Malcolm X: The Last Speeches*. New York: Pathfinder Press, 1989.

White, Florence Meiman. *Malcolm X: Black and Proud*. Champaign, Ill.: Garrard, 1975.

Williams, Juan. *Eyes on the Prize*. New York: Viking, 1987.

MAGAZINE ARTICLES

Bradley, David. "My Hero Malcolm X." *Esquire*, December 1983.

Campbell, Ray H. "Widow of Malcolm X Carries On." *The Atlanta Constitution*, July 26, 1988.

"Death of Malcolm X." *OP*, May 21, 1976.

Haley, Alex. "Alex Haley Remembers Malcolm." *Essence*, November 1983.

Hentoff, Nat. "Remembering Malcolm." *Village Voice*, February 26, 1985.

Hopkins, Ellen. "Their Fathers' Daughters." *Rolling Stone*, November 30, 1989.

"Interview with Alex Haley." *Playboy*, May 1963.

Jones, Lisa Chapman. "Talking Book." *Village Voice*, February 26, 1985.

Knebel, Fletcher. "A Visit With the Widow of Malcolm X." *Look*, Vol. 33, No. 5, March 4, 1969.

"The Legacy of Malcolm X." *Ebony*, May 1989.

Leiman, Melvin. "Malcolm X." *Liberation*, April 1965.

"The Lesson Of Malcolm X." *Saturday Evening Post*, Vol. 237, no. 31, September 12, 1964.

Lowe, Walter. "A Look Behind Malcolm X's Mask." *Sunday Star Ledger*, February 11, 1973.

Nadle, Marlene. "Malcolm X: The Complexity of a Man in the Jungle." *Village Voice*, February 25, 1965.

Perry, Bruce Frazier. "Malcolm X in Brief: A Psychological Perspective." *The Journal of Psychohistory*, Spring 1984.

Playthell, Benjamin. "Elijah, Malcolm, and Louis." *Village Voice*, August 15, 1989.

Playthell, Benjamin. "The Attitude is the Message." *Village Voice*, August 15, 1989.

Rustin, Bayard. "Making His Mark." *Sunday Herald Tribune, Book Week*. November 14, 1965.

INDEX

About the Author

Born in Cardiff, Wales, Mark Davies graduated from Cambridge University, England, with a degree in social anthropology. Since then he has worked in theater, television, children's publishing, and magazine publishing. Mr. Davies is married and lives in New York City. *Malcolm X: Another Side of the Movement* is his fourth children's book.